THE TEACHING FOR SOCIAL JUSTICE SERIES

William Ayers—*Series Editor*
Therese Quinn—*Associate Series Editor*

Editorial Board: Hal Adams, Barbara Bowman, Lisa Delpit, Michelle Fine, Maxine Greene, Caroline Heller, Annette Henry, Asa Hilliard, Rashid Khalidi, Gloria Ladson-Billings, Charles Payne, Mark Perry, Luis Rodriguez, Jonathan Silin, William Watkins

Worth Striking For: Why Education Policy Is Every Every Teacher's Concern (Lessons from Chicago)
ISABEL NUÑEZ, GREGORY MICHIE, AND PAMELA KONKOL

Being Bad:
My Baby Brother and the School-to-Prison Pipeline
CRYSTAL T. LAURA

Fear and Learning in America: Bad Data, Good Teachers, and the Attack on Public Education
JOHN KUHN

Deep Knowledge: Learning to Teach Science for Understanding and Equity
DOUGLAS B. LARKIN

Bad Teacher! How Blaming Teachers Distorts the Bigger Picture
KEVIN K. KUMASHIRO

Crossing Boundaries—
Teaching and Learning with Urban Youth
VALERIE KINLOCH

The Assault on Public Education: Confronting the Politics of Corporate School Reform
WILLIAM H. WATKINS, ED.

Pedagogy of the Poor:
Building the Movement to End Poverty
WILLIE BAPTIST & JAN REHMANN

Grow Your Own Teachers:
Grassroots Change for Teacher Education
ELIZABETH A. SKINNER, MARIA TERESA GARRETÓN, & BRIAN D. SCHULTZ, EDS.

Girl Time:
Literacy, Justice, and the School-to-Prison Pipeline
MAISHA T. WINN

Holler If You Hear Me: The Education of a Teacher and His Students, Second Edition
GREGORY MICHIE

Controversies in the Classroom:
A Radical Teacher Reader
JOSEPH ENTIN, ROBERT C. ROSEN, & LEONARD VOGT, EDS.

Spectacular Things Happen Along the Way:
Lessons from an Urban Classroom
BRIAN D. SCHULTZ

The Seduction of Common Sense: How the Right Has Framed the Debate on America's Schools
KEVIN K. KUMASHIRO

Teach Freedom: Education for Liberation in the African-American Tradition
CHARLES M. PAYNE & CAROL SILLS STRICKLAND, EDS.

Social Studies for Social Justice:
Teaching Strategies for the Elementary Classroom
RAHIMA C. WADE

Pledging Allegiance:
The Politics of Patriotism in America's Schools
JOEL WESTHEIMER, ED.

See You When We Get There:
Teaching for Change in Urban Schools
GREGORY MICHIE

Echoes of Brown: Youth Documenting and Performing the Legacy of *Brown v. Board of Education*
MICHELLE FINE

Writing in the Asylum: Student Poets in City Schools
JENNIFER MCCORMICK

Teaching the Personal and the Political:
Essays on Hope and Justice
WILLIAM AYERS

Teaching Science for Social Justice
ANGELA CALABRESE BARTON ET AL.

Putting the Children First:
The Changing Face of Newark's Public Schools
JONATHAN G. SILIN & CAROL LIPPMAN, EDS.

Refusing Racism:
White Allies and the Struggle for Civil Rights
CYNTHIA STOKES BROWN

A School of Our Own: Parents, Power, and Community at the East Harlem Block Schools
TOM RODERICK

The White Architects of Black Education:
Ideology and Power in America, 1865–1954
WILLIAM WATKINS

Worth Striking For

Why Education Policy Is Every Teacher's Concern

(Lessons from Chicago)

Isabel Nuñez | Gregory Michie | Pamela Konkol

Foreword by Pedro Noguera

TEACHERS COLLEGE PRESS

TEACHERS COLLEGE | COLUMBIA UNIVERSITY

NEW YORK AND LONDON

Published by Teachers College Press, 1234 Amsterdam Avenue, New York, NY 10027

Copyright © 2015 by Teachers College, Columbia University

Library of Congress Cataloging-in-Publication Data is available at loc.gov

ISBN 978-0-8077-5626-3 (paper)
ISBN 978-0-8077-5627-0 (hardcover)
ISBN 978-0-8077-7363-5 (ebook)

Printed on acid-free paper
Manufactured in the United States of America

22 21 20 19 18 17 16 15   8 7 6 5 4 3 2 1

Contents

Series Foreword

Teaching with Conscience in an Imperfect World

Teaching and social justice—each term is compelling and layered, each difficult to define because each is more process than precise definition, more journey than destination. *Teaching* is first of all a relationship, excruciatingly complex and wildly diverse in practice and application; and *social justice* is the striving of people in different times and places, under vastly different circumstances, using different tools and tactics to achieve greater freedom, fairness, equity, access, agency, recognition, openness, and sustainability; that striving sees the forces pressing down upon us—forces of oppression and exploitation, racism and discrimination, pestilence and plague—as unnatural and changeable.

Teaching is always practiced in a specific site, a tangible here and now, always brought to life in the mud and muck of the dynamic, surging, transient, imperfect, and fugitive world we share—this community or another, this prairie or that field, this classroom/school or that other one, this street or that street. But whatever corner of the planet we occupy, wherever we find ourselves tossed up on the shores of history, we must open our eyes if we are to make a reasonably accurate measure of the world around us.

Imagine if we had been teaching in America in the days of chattel slavery; that urgent reality—we can easily see now—would have been informative, even foundational, in everything we undertook. The peculiar institution—even when unnoticed or unacknowledged—was society's defining truth, and everyone lived in its shadow and bent to its shape one way or another. Everyone chose who to be and how to act in light of human bondage as a central fact of life.

Because "we have arrived safely here" 150 years later, it's easy to imagine we would have been brave and daring, thoughtful and effective Abolitionists in both our classrooms and our communities. We'd have taught our children about the evils of slavery, organized the Underground Railroad if we were among the free citizenry, run away if we were one of the captive Africans, helped Harriet Tubman on her journeys, and made common cause with Frederick Douglass and John Brown. Of course, had we done any of that, had we even spoken up against slavery we would have been speaking against the law and the Constitution, the Supreme Court and the Founders, the Bible and the local preacher, some neighbors and friends and most pillars of the community. But, okay, we may as well flatter ourselves now and imagine that we'd have stood up in the tradition of resistance to injustice and fighting for freedom way back then.

Of course that settles nothing for today. We still live in shadows and are still bent by our constraining systems. Slavery was ended in the United States, but descendants of Africans and the poor fill the nation's handcuffs, courtrooms, and jail cells. The abolitionists of our time imagine a world without prisons, and the work begins. Other histories emerge in the present as well, calling and challenging us: Can we finally acknowledge our colonial past, and honor our commitments to indigenous people? Will women ever be fully paid for all their work? And: What else is urgent now? What else are we not seeing? If we hope to become ethical actors in our own society, we need to make every effort to pay attention, to open our eyes again and again, and to try to sort out those things that are fair and just and beneficial for the world from those that are unjust or terrible and therefore unacceptable—even if customary, conventional, authorized and legal; even when completely expected.

Paying attention is the starting point of ethical action, but it is not the end. We need to allow ourselves to be astonished at the loveliness all around as well as the appalling injustices everywhere. We need to be astounded and angry at the pain we visit upon one another, and then we must speak up and act out about whatever the known demands of us. Pay attention; be astonished; act—that's the rhythm of moral thought, and add the need to doubt that whatever you did or said was adequate. Start over at the beginning: pay attention, be astonished, act, and doubt. Repeat for a lifetime. If we are to live fully, deeply, purposefully, we need to get busy here and now.

We don't choose the world as such; rather we are thrust into a world already here, up and running. We hurry to catch up, taking the world as it is to start, unvarnished, and plunging forward as participants and accomplices toward the new and the unknown. We can choose to try to change the world for the better, but we must do so in circumstances not at all of our own choosing. If we are keeping our eyes and ears open, we'll find many places to get started; if we keep our hearts open we will find that partners for this work are all around.

As teachers we acknowledge a profound truth: Standing side by side with the world as such—the world we see and smell and feel and engage—is a possible world, a world that could be or should be, but is not here yet. That feasible world, that alternative space, is pregnant with potential and promise, and it beckons to us and points toward an enlarged horizon. Our imaginations are called into service in the classroom, and questions emerge: What are we? Where do we come from? How did we get here? Where do we want to go? This is the territory of the mind's eye and the heart's desire. This is where we enliven our values and enact our ethical judgments.

What makes education in a democracy distinct from education under a dictatorship or a monarchy is a commitment to a particularly precious and fragile ideal: Every human being is of infinite and incalculable value, each a unique intellectual, emotional, physical, spiritual, and creative force. This tells us that the fullest development of all is the necessary condition for the full development of each, and, conversely, the fullest development of each is necessary for the full development of all. Imagine enacting this in our schools and classrooms, really embracing it and carrying it forward in every interaction.

As teachers we encourage students to develop initiative and imagination, the capacity to name the world, to identify the obstacles to their full humanity, and the courage to act upon whatever the known demands. Education in a democracy is characteristically eye-popping and mind-blowing—always about opening doors and opening minds as students forge their own pathways into a wider, shared world.

Much of what we call schooling forecloses or shuts down or walls off meaningful choice-making. Much of it is based on obedience and conformity, the hallmarks of every authoritarian regime throughout history. Much of it banishes the unpopular, squirms in the presence of the unorthodox, hides the unpleasant. There's no space for skepticism, irreverence, or even doubt. While many of us long for teaching as something transcendent and powerful, we find ourselves too often locked in situations that reduce teaching to a kind of glorified clerking, passing along a curriculum of received wisdom and predigested and often false bits of information. This is a recipe for disaster in the long run.

Educators, students, residents and citizens might press now for an education worthy of a democracy, including an end to sorting people into winners and losers through expensive standardized tests which act as pseudo-scientific forms of surveillance; an end to starving schools of needed resources and then blaming teachers for dismal outcomes; and an end to the rapidly accumulating "educational debt," the resources due to communities historically segregated, under-funded and underserved. All children and youth in a democracy, regardless of economic circumstance, deserve full access to richly resourced classrooms led by caring, qualified, and generously compensated teachers. Whatever the wisest and most privileged parents want for their kids—that is exactly where we begin as a community sketching out what we want for all of our children.

Education at its best is an enterprise geared toward allowing every human being to reach a fuller measure of her or his humanity. It's the irreducible and incalculable value of every human life linked to the teacherly work of unlocking and releasing the power of each person that gives the work of teaching its fundamental shape and direction.

A teaching identity is built in the cauldron of a classroom—from the very start focus laser-like on a group of youngsters: How do they learn? What are their preferences? If they could choose, what would they do? What strengths and interests do they bring with them into the classroom? How could these be built upon and made into bridges toward deeper and wider ways of knowing? Could conversation about large goals and ethical purposes productively power life in school? More than any textbook or theory, more than adherence to a specific philosophy or ideology, we invent and re-invent ourselves as teachers through these kinds of questions, and our students become the essential co-creators.

Guided by an unshakable belief in the incalculable value of every human being, we begin to improvise. We might split the large group up—to everyone's advantage. We might bring in lots of books, lots of art supplies and quirky stuff, and let the students choose. We might not like ourselves—or even recognize ourselves—as tightly wound task-masters and petty dictators, so we loosen up and slow down, and learn how to be with students in a more authentic way, more alive in our own enthusiasms and preferences and responses. Our classrooms may become homes away from home, our students, family.

All children need to develop a sense of the unique capacity of human beings to shape and create reality in concert with conscious purposes and plans. This means that our schools need to be transformed to provide children ongoing opportunities to exercise their resourcefulness, to solve the real problems of their communities. Like all human beings, children and young people need to be of use—they cannot productively be treated as "objects" to be taught "subjects." Their cognitive juices will begin to flow if and when their hearts, heads, and hands are engaged in improving their daily lives and their surroundings.

This ethical core is as well the political stance of an independent, thoughtful, and caring teacher: No power is too big to challenge, no injustice too small to ignore. We can be markedly on the side of profound, fundamental change, the kind of upheaval that would replace greed and repression and hierarchy and surveillance and control with community, peace, simple fairness, and love—all kinds of love for all kinds of people in every situation. The radical message is simply: choose love.

—William Ayers & Therese Quinn

Foreword

Over the last several years, education has become a highly visible and polarized political issue. Even as the nation has grappled with a host of other pressing and at times intractable issues—war, disease, climate change, home foreclosures, etc., education has not receded in importance as a policy issue worth fighting for. Much of the attention is due to the efforts of policymakers, philanthropists, and corporate leaders who have moved aggressively to *reform* public education. For the most part, they have sought to do this through standards-based accountability (i.e., high-stakes testing) and a number of market-based reforms (e.g., expanding the number of charter schools, evaluating teachers based on student test scores, closing schools regarded as "failing").

Teachers have been noticeably absent from the debate over the direction and the future of public education. This is not because teachers don't have opinions on these issues but simply because they typically don't have access to the megaphone, platform, or airwaves to be heard. Sadly, in the absence of well-developed arguments and perspectives from teachers, education policy and reform are being determined largely by people who know very little about education. In the United States today, those who know the least about education have the most say, and those who know the most have almost no say at all.

With funding from some of the nation's wealthiest individuals and political backing from the Bush and Obama administrations, a new generation of reformers has gained the upper hand in policy debates. In cities like New Orleans, Washington, DC, and Detroit, they have been able to remake entire school systems, closing traditional public schools and replacing them with charter schools. They have been able to convince (some would suggest bribe) states across the country to adopt sweeping new policy measures such as the Common Core Learning Standards and new teacher evaluation plans, without any evidence that these measures will deliver the progress promised. They have marginalized parents, spent billions of dollars on untested ideas (e.g., iPads, small schools, and data-based accountability systems), and with advocates like former New York City Chancellor Joel Klein and former DC Chancellor Michelle Rhee taking the lead they have been able to portray the opposition to their ideas as "defenders of the status quo."

Yet, despite their overwhelming dominance due to almost unlimited funding and media coverage, opposition to the new reform agenda has grown, and teachers are increasingly at the forefront. Signs of pushback are taking many forms, but like flowers in springtime they have begun sprouting throughout the country. In New York, the election of progressive mayor Bill de Blasio, who campaigned in open opposition to former mayor Mike Bloomberg's embrace of market-based reform, was seen by many as a clear repudiation of his predecessor's education policies. Similarly, the election of pro-union school board members in Los Angeles who won citywide races despite being outspent by reform advocates, and the election of principal Ras Baraka in Newark who openly opposed the market-based reforms championed by his predecessor Cory Booker, are all signs that the tide may be changing. In several states and cities there is a growing movement to opt out of standardized testing led by teachers, parents, and students. Finally, groups across the country have been organizing to put a stop to school closures that have disproportionately impacted poor Black and Latino communities in Philadelphia, New York, and Oakland.

Undoubtedly, the most powerful sign of opposition to the reform agenda emerged in Chicago during the teachers' strike of 2012. In that city a newly elected progressive union leadership challenged mayor Rahm Emanuel's attempt to ram through a package of measures that were seen as harmful to teachers and students. Rather than merely focusing on salaries and benefits, the union boldly embraced a larger reform agenda of their own that included reduced class sizes; a "better" school day enriched by music, art, and physical education; and fair compensation and evaluations. The CTU (Chicago Teachers Union) understood that the strike was a risky move. By effectively shutting down schools the union risked alienating and even angering parents. However, in a sign of their political awareness and sophistication, CTU members went to great lengths to obtain parent support by organizing an extensive campaign to educate them about the issues. The strategy worked. During the 8-day strike parents marched with teachers and polls showed overwhelming public support for the teachers' demands.

Worth Striking For, written by teachers who have been at the forefront of the battle to stop market-based reform, is yet another step in the effort to reclaim the reform agenda.

It goes beyond the strike to explore teacher perspectives on a broader set of education policy issues, and in so doing it elevates the voices of teachers in a way that few publications or arenas have allowed. The authors do more than offer a pointed critique of mayor Rahm Emanuel and his plans; they systematically examine what is at stake for teachers, students, and American democracy as the effort to privatize public education advances. By linking their analysis to a thoughtful discussion of the purpose of education in a society that is being rapidly transformed by racial segregation and rising inequality, they bring a perspective to the future of American education that for too long has been missing.

Since the nation's governors got together in 1983 to issue *A Nation at Risk*, a report that decried America's growing mediocrity in education, reforms have been carried out in a top-down manner (led by former Arkansas Governor Bill Clinton). Powerful politicians, corporate elites, and philanthropists have defined the problem and conceived of solutions to "fix" America's schools typically without ever consulting the people who work there. More often than not urban schools, populated primarily by low-income children of color, have been the targets of these reform measures. High dropout rates, low test scores, and lagging performance on international assessments have been used as the justification for the remedies they have prescribed. Though they have buttressed their appeals for change with a call for data-based accountability, they have been remarkably reluctant to hold themselves accountable for the results obtained in schools where their policies have been applied.

The elites driving the current reform agenda have been imposing changes upon schools that are driving many teachers out of the profession. It is time for teachers and their allies to push back. *Worth Striking For* is a timely and much-needed response from teachers to the assault on public education. Let's hope that there will be much more to come from those on the front lines of defending public education.

—Pedro Noguera

Introduction:
Keep a Place for Policy

Teaching can be all-consuming—and we mean this in the best possible way. Each of the authors of this book has taught in public schools—elementary, middle, and high school—and one of us (Gregory Michie) just two years ago returned to the classroom. We all know how intense the work of teaching is—and how rewarding. Sure, there are stacks of papers to grade and tedious paperwork to complete, but most of what keeps teachers busy is joyful, passionate engagement with the students, the subject matter, and the synergy forged in bringing the two together. Each young life encountered is worth contemplating at length: Who is this human being? Where might he or she find joy and fulfillment, and what can I do to help? Content at any level—from a penguin theme in an early childhood classroom to a high school English teacher's favorite novel for sharing with 11th-grade students—is a bottomless source of revelation for educators who are open to learning with their students.

Then there is the teaching itself, the art and the science equally absorbing. Pedagogy is the ultimate subject for lifelong learning, rewarding research into methodological breakthroughs, and even closer study of the unique learning needs and interests of the individuals before you. Seeing the excitement in students' faces when they grasp a challenging concept is a visceral pleasure, celebratory and electric. There is a different kind of pleasure than in the earlier "a-ha" moment when the lesson plan comes together and you know what you need to do to get the group to that place.

It may seem counterintuitive, but the intensity doesn't subside as the years go on. When I, Isabel, was teaching 1st grade, each year I spent more hours planning and preparing than in the previous year, because each year I could see more clearly how I could do my job better. It seems funny that as teaching got "easier" (as I

1

felt more comfortable and confident in my work), it actually took more time and effort. Eventually I became one of those teachers for whom their work is nearly their whole life and identity—not a path I necessarily recommend, but an understandable one when diving into such an enriching and inspiring vocation.

In spite of all of this—and acknowledging just how busy teachers are—we have something critically important to recommend in this book: Set aside some time and space for policy. We know that it doesn't have the immediacy of some of the issues teachers face on a day-to-day basis, and we know that the topic isn't as sexy or fun as some of the other areas where excess professional energy might be spent—if such excess indeed exists. Yet, from our all-consuming classrooms in Los Angeles and Chicago, each of us somehow found our way to the Center for Policy Studies and Social Justice at Concordia University Chicago. This is not because we are boring people by nature—we truly wish education policy were unproblematic enough to be boring. We felt compelled. In the past couple of decades, the landscape of public education has changed so dramatically that there was no choice. The classroom contexts in which we began our careers don't exist anymore. If teachers do not have a voice in U.S. education policy, there may no longer be a vocation of teaching.

THE CHICAGO TEACHERS' STRIKE OF 2012

In the summer of 2012, one city's teachers did have a voice. After a tough year of contract negotiations between the Chicago Teachers Union (CTU) and the Chicago Public Schools (CPS), the teachers eventually came to the difficult decision to go on strike for the first time in 25 years. Interestingly, 21 of those years had been under former Chicago Mayor Richard M. Daley, who, for all of the damage he did to the public schools, maintained cordial relationships with the city's public-sector workers. The newly elected mayor, Rahm Emanuel, seemed to be taking a very different approach, fighting the union at every turn.

Perhaps his intransigence felt safe after the Illinois legislature passed legislation stating that authorization of a strike required agreement of at least 75% of teachers union members—a law that was designed to be debilitating to teachers unions. Jonah Edelman,

CEO of the "astroturf" (referring to an organization masquerading as grassroots that is actually well funded from outside sources) reform group Stand for Children, bragged at a festival in Aspen just a year prior that he'd succeeded in ensuring that the Chicago Teachers Union would never strike. He claimed to have outwitted CTU president Karen Lewis, whom he presumed did not know the history of voting patterns. It turns out that she knew her teachers. More than 90% of Chicago teachers voted in June to authorize a strike.

For parents with work and other obligations, a teachers' strike is no easy thing to accommodate, so both the CTU and CPS got early messages out, each hoping to persuade families that, if worse came to worst and a strike were to happen, the other side would be the one at fault. After then-CPS CEO Jean-Claude Brizard sent parents a letter—via CPS teachers and students—presenting the authorization vote as premature and counterproductive to the negotiation process, Lewis and the union responded with a letter of their own. While reassuring parents that an authorization vote would not make a strike a certainty, the letter explained what the two sides were stuck on. In a bulleted list, Lewis presented the union's key demands:

- Smaller classes
- A better day to go with a longer day
- Fair compensation
- Job security

These were the key issues that Chicago teachers deemed to be the heart of the matter, and perhaps even worthy of striking over. To be sure, where a district falls in relation to each of these affects a teacher's day-to-day work tremendously. In addition, since teachers' working conditions are students' learning conditions, Lewis is correct in pointing out in the letter that "these demands are aligned with the interests of parents and children." However, each of these also is closely related to broader shifts in education policy that have taken place over the past decade or so, and to the diverse and sometimes conflicting purposes of schooling as envisioned by different individuals during different periods in U.S. history. Each will be discussed in Chapter 2.

Smaller classes enable the supportive learning communities

and personal relationships between teachers and students that nurture young people in fully exploring their interests, intellects, and talents—so they can grow up to contribute fully to our democratic society. The better day, explained in the letter as a curriculum that includes art, world languages, and P.E., ensures that schools are able to transmit the rich cultural heritage of the United States, rather than being limited to a narrow band of skills in reading and math. A concern for social efficiency would demand that teachers be fairly compensated, if we want the most talented individuals to choose teaching as a career. If the purpose of schooling is to facilitate social change, rather than a more efficient status quo, teachers need to be secure in their jobs so they can continue to push for progress in the face of inevitable resistance.

THE POLICY IMPLICATIONS

The CTU's four demands, and the philosophical purposes of schooling that they concretize, are each connected to a particular sphere of education policy. The public policy realm as a whole has undergone rapid and radical change in recent years, with perhaps no policy structure as thoroughly revised as that of our public schools. All four ways of envisioning the educational project—preparation for democratic participation, transmission of a cultural tradition, an efficient and effective society, and the impetus for social change—have been strengthened or compromised by various shifts in policy, sometimes by the same policy. And all of these changes, of course, have had real-world implications for teachers and students, families and communities.

In this book, we discuss what we feel have been the most significant shifts in education policy of the past decade or so. These are presented in their relationship to the lived experiences of real teachers in real classrooms, but also in the ways that they help or hinder schools with regard to broader educational purposes. The next chapter presents a brief history of the Chicago teachers' strike of 2012, as well as some background on the different ways education has been understood in the United States. Each of the following four chapters describes one of the Chicago teachers' demands, and then explores a related policy arena through the lens of an associated philosophical purpose of education. The chapters also include individually authored vignettes that present our personal experiences with the issues in the text, and they end with a list of suggested titles for further reading.

Chapter 2, "Chicago Teachers United," tells the story of the Chicago teachers' strike. In it we narrate the sights, sounds, and public conversations of the time, and also provide some background on the issues then facing the Chicago education community—many of which we trust will be familiar to readers in other parts of the country. We provide a historical view of the shift in union leadership and priorities that made the labor action possible. The chapter explains what teachers were officially entitled to strike for, and what their real concerns were—as well as the legislation that made these discrepant. We describe the policy outcomes of the strike, its accomplishments as well as what it failed to achieve. We close this locally focused chapter with a broader view, considering in turn each of four approaches to conceptualizing the enterprise of education. These four perspectives on the purpose of schools—to enhance democracy, to instill a common culture, to facilitate social efficiency, and to inspire social change—each have important policy manifestations, which are explored in the chapters to follow.

In Chapter 3, "Students, Teachers, and Schools," we consider the Chicago Teachers Union's demand for smaller class sizes. Smaller classes have been definitively shown to improve achievement, especially for African American and low-income students. More important, this concern on the part of the union reflects the philosophical belief that the purpose of education is to serve democracy, an aim that requires the full development and flourishing of every student, which is possible only when teachers can engage with them individually. This chapter has three subsections addressing recent policy shifts that weaken schools' ability to serve this purpose.

Culturally and Linguistically Diverse Learners. From the renaming of the federal Office of Bilingual Education to the Office of English Acquisition, to the quiet disappearance of or targeted attacks on multicultural education, schools have moved away from nurturing the differences that make for a vibrant democracy. In states such as California and Arizona, where education policy has been made by referendum, teaching a student in his or her native language is now against the law.

School Integration. Housing segregation traditionally has been blamed for the difficulty in achieving the integrated schools mandated by *Brown v. Board of Education*. Yet, the very school choice policies that once seemed promising with regard to lessening segregation in fact have exacerbated it. Chapter 3 examines how recent reforms further isolate poor and minority students.

Diversity of the Teaching Force. A variety of policy shifts have resulted in a Whiter, more middle-class teaching force in the past several years. Higher cut scores for licensing exams have made it more difficult for Black and Latino candidates (traditionally ill-served by standardized tests) to enter the field. The closures of schools in struggling communities have disproportionately impacted non-White veteran teachers.

Chapter 4, "Curriculum and Pedagogy," begins with Chicago Mayor Rahm Emanuel's push for a longer school day, which dates back to his election campaign. The city's teachers responded with the demand that the day be not just longer, but better. The arts, world languages, and physical education are just a few of the curricular areas that have suffered in the intensifying focus on test scores—primarily in reading and math. The newly narrowed curriculum is also more tightly controlled, with teachers being told not just what to teach, but how to teach it. In this chapter we consider the issues in light of another historical goal of schooling in society—the introduction to a shared cultural tradition. While this goal is in some ways served by recent policy shifts, in other ways it is not.

Testing. Tests allow us to make limited inferences about student learning; however, they should never be the sole gauge. Yet, the equation of test scores with student learning, and the framing of "accountability" around whether teachers are doing their jobs, have led to an almost completely test-driven curriculum in many schools and classrooms. This has led to a dramatic decline in breadth and depth of student engagement with U.S., Western, and world cultural traditions.

Common Core. While proponents argue that the new Common Core State Standards are the best means through which our shared culture as a nation can be preserved and passed down, the continuation of high-stakes and low-cost testing is as likely to result in a shallow level of engagement with those traditions. Also, we are in danger of losing the opportunity for the innovative, creative teacher/student-developed curricula that have enabled U.S. cultural traditions to flourish.

Teacher Deskilling. Curriculum design is just one area that is being taken from the hands of classroom teachers. The deprofessionalization of teaching can be traced from top-down control of teaching practices to the forced use of scripted curricula, from the prevalence in some areas of Teach for America–style novices in the classroom to proposals in some states that teachers need not have college degrees.

In Chapter 5, "Funding and Governance," we examine the third demand of Chicago's striking teachers, a central issue in most labor disputes and a perennial challenge for teachers in particular: fair compensation. For the many people who conceptualize the purpose of schooling as facilitating social efficiency, this demand is understandable. In a market-based economy, the priority given to any enterprise is reflected in the resources devoted to it. In other words, if teachers' work is important, it must be well paid. In this chapter, we examine issues of funding and governance through the lens of resource maximization, which many reforms seem outwardly to serve.

School Funding. Since the 1973 Supreme Court decision that held it constitutional to fund schools through local property taxes, the matter appeared to have been settled. However, it is worthwhile to consider whether the benefits of schooling flow only to the local community or are shared by society as a whole. Differences in funding formulas between states also are examined fruitfully as evidence of diverse positions on how social efficiency is best served.

School Accountability. The widely repeated narrative on schools' lack of accountability, itself open to debate, often is used to justify the further underresourcing of an already overburdened system. Worse, it is presented as a reason to remove the enterprise of education from the public sector altogether. While an abiding faith in the market may well be the motivation for many who make this argument, the evidence suggests that it is already moving public money into private hands without improving educational outcomes for children in the United States.

Top-Down Control. It is probably not a coincidence that this transfer of wealth has happened alongside an increasing concentration of power at the top of school systems—and sometimes out of the hands of educators altogether. The work of teachers, once self-directed, has come under closer scrutiny from school and district-level administrators, whose own decisions are guided by appointed boards or, as in Chicago, by the mayor himself.

Chapter 6, "The Vocation of Teaching," is inspired by what may be the most controversial of the demands of the Chicago teachers: job security. When teachers defend tenure (now a highly endangered provision under Race to the Top), they are likely to hear, "Well, *I* don't have any guarantees with regard to *my* job," from fellow workers in the private sector. Such ire seems misdirected, as workers on the whole would be better off if more, rather than less, of the labor force could have job security. The reason this right has been institutionalized for teachers is the recognition of the unique role they have with regard to a fourth purpose of schooling: to inspire and facilitate social change. Teacher tenure is under increasing threat, as we have seen unprecedented attacks on the vocation of teaching.

Value-Added Measures in Teacher Evaluation. The confluence of high-stakes testing and calls for accountability has resulted in an unimaginably destructive approach to evaluating teachers, one that will mean regular random turnover in the profession. While there is a commonsense appeal to using test scores to rate teachers—if one makes the mistake of equating scores with learning—the statistical models that now exist are so riven with error that the largest professional bodies of statisticians, mathematicians, economists, public policy experts, and psychometricians (the people who know the math) have all denounced the practice, which is nevertheless law in many states.

Teachers Unions. The vilification of teachers generally has been especially vehement where teachers unions are concerned, and many in the public conversation have latched on to the story of unions' primary purpose being to keep bad teachers in the classroom. However, the proliferation of charter schools, which are not required to hire union teachers, provides a predictive picture of the most likely outcomes should teachers unions be destroyed: rapid turnover of overworked and undercompensated teachers.

Public Schooling. The ultimate goal of the current reform efforts around education policy appears to be the end to our public system of schooling, whether motivated by true faith in the market or by desire for new profit-making opportunities. There are many populations that have not been well served by schools in the United States, and an understandable urgency exists on the part of many to try something different. However, any and all shifts in vision and/or policy for the U.S. educational system need to be the subject of vigorous and informed debate, especially on the part of teachers.

The concluding chapter, "The Need for a Politically Engaged Teaching Force," reminds us that, while each of them is important enough to strike for, the stated demands of Chicago's teachers do not tell the whole story. Legislation designed to weaken the unions had limited the issues about which teachers could strike to compensation and working conditions, as well as requiring the 75% approval noted earlier. The struggle was about far more than the four demands laid out by Karen Lewis in her letter to parents. Teachers were defending students, families, and communities. As was evident in September when the teachers eventually did go on strike, this is something that parents understood well. When teachers are informed about how education policy intersects with local community issues, and they are vocal in advocating the policies that best serve families, students, and schools, they can build the kind of momentum that made Chicago into, as a CTU report (Noonan, Farmer, & Huckaby, 2014) describes, "a sea of red."

WHEN TEACHERS TAKE A STAND

Despite the hardships endured by families over the 8 days of the teachers' strike—and these were substantial—the parents of Chicago Public Schools stood behind children, and behind their teachers. Polls of city residents showed most people backing the teachers, with even stronger majorities among African American and Latino Chicagoans, who were most likely to be CPS parents. Fellow public-sector employees were loud in their support, and "Proud Union Home" lawn signs popped up all over the city and suburbs. The teachers of Chicago, in taking a stand on education policy, found that they were joined by the voice of the public. It was this collective voice of teachers and residents—the handmade signs, the honking and cheering as people passed the rallies and picket lines—that made Mayor Emanuel sit up and take notice. And it was the city and the teachers together who earned the concessions of the final contract, which included some gains with regard to each of the four demands.

Of course, the renegotiated contract and the end of the strike did not mean the end of the fight over school policy in Chicago. If anything, it has intensified with the closing of 49 schools at the end of the academic year that began with the strike. This was also met with fierce resistance by the Chicago Teachers Union, organized parents, and others in the city, who did succeed in reducing the original number of 80 planned closures. Still, it was a difficult spring to be in Chicago—as painful as the fall was joyful. We will not win every battle in the education policy arena, but each of our efforts will make a difference.

All teachers must recognize that decisions about education policy affect not only their work and livelihoods, but the workforce participation and life chances of the young people in front of them every day. When parents also grasp what is at stake when policy is being debated, they are powerful allies. The voices of teachers and parents, when joined together, have the potential to shape the larger public conversation about education, which for too long has been dominated by corporate interests and venture philanthropists (Saltman, 2010). A collective voice in support of public education can raise the debate from the false certainty of test-score-based accountability to the loftier visions held for U.S. schools in generations past.

This is the responsibility of teachers, as the individuals who know most intimately the implications of both positive and destructive changes in policy. There is much that will make it difficult, from the time-intensive nature of teaching to the constant questioning of educators' motives in resisting ill-conceived policies, but *all* teachers must become politically aware and actively engaged. If this does not become an integral part of teachers' work, there soon may be no vocation of teaching.

Chicago Teachers United

This past decade has been an especially difficult time to be an educator. Expectations of teachers have been high since the early years of our nation, when young female normal school graduates were held up as moral exemplars to the communities in which they taught, and morality was understood to mean they were not permitted to marry—or even to be seen in public with male non-relatives (Spring, 2013). While teachers are still expected to model societal conceptions of good character—hence the "moral turpitude clauses" in many districts' teacher contracts and the Texas Administrative Code (Code of Ethics and Standard Practice for Texas Educators, 2010)—much more has been added to the list of our responsibilities.

As education budgets are slashed from the federal to the district level, classroom teachers are required to take on the roles of counselors, school nurses, art and music teachers, social workers, and other former colleagues whose positions have been eliminated. Worse, teachers have been blamed for the economic conditions precipitating the budget cuts (so really, we are told, this is our own fault!). In addition, as Leonie Haimson of Class Size Matters (a nonprofit clearinghouse) observes, "Across the country, class sizes are increasing at unprecedented rates" (Strauss, 2010b)—yet another way that teachers' work has been intensified. As has been intoned from the presidential pulpit (Obama, 2010) to the television pundits to dinner tables across the United States, schools need to play a major role in rebuilding the country's economy. If this wasn't a heavy enough load to bear, teachers also have been handed responsibility for the precarious state of U.S. national security, with the Council on Foreign Relations claiming in a report that poor schools are putting Americans' safety at risk (Klein & Rice, 2012).

THE STORY OF THE STRIKE

Chicago teachers in the years before the 2012 strike were feeling
the weight of all the extra expectations being shouldered by their
colleagues across the country, as well as the additional pressures of
teaching in a highly segregated, poverty-intensive city that has been
a flash point for radical changes to the way schools are organized,
run, and even conceptualized in the United States. Chicago, with its
long history of very powerful municipal executives, was one of the
earliest sites of mayoral takeover and subsequent control of a city's
schools. The 1995 Chicago School Reform Act gave sweeping power
to then-Mayor Richard M. Daley, but historian James Carl (2009)
argues that this merely codified the "mayoral authority to appoint
members of the board of education over the course of the twentieth
century [which] makes the Windy City something of a laboratory
of mayoral control" (p. 326). In keeping with that century-long history, Daley and later Mayor Rahm Emanuel have maintained the
practice of "embrac[ing] educational positions that were as much
about marshaling votes and winning the support of corporate Chicago as they were about improving the schools" (p. 326).

In recent years, this "historically cozy relationship between
the mayor's office and corporate Chicago" (Carl, 2009, p. 326) has
moved from old-fashioned patronage to the large-scale reshaping of
the educational enterprise. The Commercial Club of Chicago (representing the largest corporations in the city) designed for Mayor
Daley an outline of these changes, called the Renaissance 2010
plan. It has been described as an openly pro-business program that
is at its core "a privatization scheme for creating a 'market' in public education" (Saltman, 2010, p. 151). The chief executive officer
(CEO)—previously called the superintendent—chosen by Daley
for the Chicago Public Schools, Arne Duncan, enthusiastically directed the plan's implementation before being tapped as President
Barack Obama's secretary of education in 2008 (and spreading this
approach to "reform" nationwide). In Chicago, as a result, dozens
of neighborhood schools were closed and replaced by charter, contract, and "performance" schools, most of which employed non-
union teachers.

However, the "Renaissance" plan isn't all that is notable about
the year 2010 in the history of education in Chicago. That is also
the year that the Caucus of Rank-and-File Educators (CORE) won

the election for leadership of the Chicago Teachers Union. In a sense, the two phenomena are interdependent, as it was the tepid response of the union under former president Marilyn Stewart to school closures and turnarounds that inspired CORE's founders to form a caucus and field candidates for office (Uetricht, 2014). Teachers, activists, and scholars who gathered to study works of political and economic theory, like Naomi Klein's *The Shock Doctrine* (Uetricht, 2014, p. 33), the CORE members demonstrated a very different idea of what a teachers union is and does from the campaign forward.

The energy, enthusiasm, and organizing know-how displayed by the fledgling caucus have made the story of CORE and the CTU an exemplar for unions everywhere (Labor Notes, 2014). As a publication of the union's own research center explains, the CTU under CORE moved away from being a "service union," modeled after a business where the members are the customers, and toward a "social organizing model of unionism," where the organization's source of strength is the solidarity that will enable collective action (Noonan et al., 2014, pp. 1–2). The focus moved from individual teachers' workplace issues to the big picture, and union members came to see that their concerns were shared with one another and with the communities they served. A massive effort to educate and mobilize teachers by visiting as many schools as possible, speaking and distributing literature (Labor Notes, 2014), led to CORE's taking 60% of the vote in a runoff election against the incumbent union leadership (Uetricht, 2014).

And this was not the end of the organizing effort. The new leadership immediately began overhauling the way the union was run, cutting staff salaries to match teachers' pay and using the additional funds to hire full-time organizers to educate members on school and community issues (Uetricht, 2014). The outreach efforts sought not only to inform teachers but also to invite dialogue and, most important, to promote a shift from thinking about the union as a separate entity to thinking about it as the membership itself, as "us, we are the union" (Noonan et al., 2014, p. 8). In contrast to the previous administration's glossy magazine with photographs of social events, the new publication was less expensively produced but much more informative on the political situation facing the schools. In addition, the union released research reports and communicated through frequent email and telephone updates.

Decisionmaking was conspicuously democratic and transparent, contributing to the feeling that the members were the union. As a result, when contract negotiations turned contentious in the run-up to September 2012, Chicago's teachers were a politically savvy and unified force.

The corporate-driven movement for education "reform" also had been working hard to prepare for the new contract, the first under Mayor Emanuel. While his predecessor Mayor Daley had maintained cordial relations with public-sector unions even while implementing changes favorable to business interests (Carl, 2009), Emanuel neither claimed nor demonstrated any allegiance to the labor groups that had helped keep Chicago—and the state of Illinois—reliably Democratic. He likely felt he didn't need to; after all, the corporate "reform" movement had good reason to believe that the crippling of the teachers union was imminent.

In 2011, the Illinois legislature passed Senate Bill 7, the law that was touted by "reform" group leader Jonah Edelman as an annihilating blow to the Chicago Teachers Union because of its requirement that 75% of a union's membership must vote to approve a strike. This wasn't the only way the legislation hindered teachers from striking. Now, only the bread-and-butter issues of compensation and benefits (along with some areas of evaluation) could legally be the basis for a strike (Uetricht, 2014). In effect, teachers could strike *only* for reasons that would be sure to play in the media as selfish—their own wages and jobs. In addition to the seemingly insurmountable margin required to authorize a strike, the mayor expected that the public opinion battle would be un-winnable for the union when so restricted on the issues.

However, the importance of the upcoming contract negotiations was apparent to both sides, and the newly unified Chicago teaching force was gearing up as well. Union-led education and outreach efforts had ensured that teachers understood their conflict with the Chicago Public Schools in the broader context of the nation-wide—even worldwide—movement to reform public education in the interests of private capital (Noonan et al., 2014). The teachers understood that this was a struggle in which they and the working-class families they served in city schools should be on the same side, and they had built the relationships with individual and organized parents and community members that garnered their support when the strike came to pass. Because teachers had made the effort to get out into the neighborhoods, parents knew from the start that the union was concerned with the funding inequalities, school actions, and segregation that had been compromising the quality of education in their communities for generations. The union kept parents up-to-date on the progress of negotiations, countering a CPS message on the strike authorization vote with their own letter, sent to students' homes, explaining the significance of the vote and the issues still being debated.

In addition to its own research efforts in the CTU Quest Center, the union drew on the work of academic researchers for evidence-backed arguments that could be used in the negotiations and the media campaign. A longstanding issue—perhaps even the catalyst for the birth of CORE in the first place (Uetricht, 2014)—was teacher job losses in school "turnarounds," through which underperforming schools were given over wholly to new leadership and the entire staff was fired. A February 2012 report from research/policy group Designs for Change found that despite infusions of additional funds, such schools showed far worse results than demographically comparable but democratically governed schools. Mayor Emanuel's attempt to substantially lengthen the school day with no additional compensation for teachers was countered with an April 2012 report from the University of Illinois at Urbana-Champaign's Labor Education Program showing that Chicago teachers were already working an average of 58 hours a week while school was in session (Bruno, Ashby, & Manzo, 2012). In March 2012, a group of 88 university-based educational researchers from the metropolitan area signed a letter warning CPS against a planned early and expanded implementation of test-score-based teacher evaluation because of the many concerns raised by the research evidence (CReATE, 2012). On the latter two points, the union would claim victory after the strike.

In the media, teachers repeated the mantra "teachers' working conditions are students' learning condition" (Noonan et al., 2014, p. 11), successfully communicating the fact that the strike was about far more than money. Mayor Emanuel railed in response, condemning the strike as illegal because "the issues are not financial" (quoted in Goudie, 2012), a claim that the union did not overtly refute. The signs teachers carried while picketing and during rallies demonstrated to the public what their motivations for striking were: educational quality and educational equity (Lipman

& Gutstein, 2013). In response, the city of Chicago, in large part, stood behind its teachers. A majority of residents supported the strike. More significant, however, much larger majorities of Black and Latino Chicagoans (who are most likely to be the parents of children attending public schools) expressed support for the striking teachers (Uetricht, 2014).

It was clear that CORE's organizing and outreach efforts had paid off in yet another campaign. The patience and goodwill of parents in making other arrangements for their children, and the overwhelmingly positive public response at rallies and outside schools—not to mention the "Proud Union Home" signs popping up on lawns all over the city and suburbs—were likely instrumental in enabling teachers to pressure the district into key concessions. When the negotiating teams reached a tentative agreement, the union's commitment to democratic principles meant continuing the strike for 2 additional days so that the entire membership could read and discuss the document. This left the media in a quandary: After CTU President Karen Lewis was maligned as a heavy-handed union "boss" who'd bullied the teachers into striking, she was criticized for not being able to control her members. Meanwhile, teachers gathered on athletic field bleachers, reading and discussing the contract page by page. The CTU eventually secured a contract that was framed as a union victory in the media, despite its many compromises on both sides (Pearson, 2012).

The teachers did receive raises, although not in the amounts requested. Merit pay, which the mayor had fought for, was absent from the contract. The lengthened school day remained, but with additional compensation. The percentage of a teacher's evaluation to be based on student test scores was scaled back to the statutory minimum (already a whopping 30%). An attempted increase of 40% in teacher contributions to their health plans disappeared from the contract, but the union lost on protections for teachers displaced because of school closures. In less than a year, this would prove to be a devastating contract loss as the concession rendered affordable the district's decision to close a record-breaking number of neighborhood schools.

Still, the most important union gains from the strike may not be in the terms of the contract, and may not have been won either at the bargaining table or on the picket lines. The work for these victories began even before CORE took over the reins of the CTU, in the reading and thinking and discussion that eventually led to the formation of the caucus. From this philosophical vision work came an intellectually grounded commitment to activism. This energy was put to use in the campaign for union leadership, and then in the political education of the broader union membership. These efforts enabled the union to collect strike votes from 90% of its members during summer vacation and inspired 98% of them to vote yes. This work laid the foundation on which thousands of teachers marched in fire-engine-red union T-shirts through the streets of Chicago, creating "a sea of red" (Noonan et al., 2014). The reward, cemented by the experience of the strike itself, is an empowered teaching force no longer feeling helpless in the face of corporate efforts to privatize education. Chicago's teachers, along with its mayor and district leaders, have learned that resistance is possible, that the public is supportive, and that we do not have to give up our schools without a fight.

The Chicago Teachers Union also strengthened the relationships with parents and community groups that can be the basis for united efforts to reinstate democratic control of public education. In the spring of 2014, the city got a taste of what the combined power of teachers and parents might look like, when significant numbers of both groups took a stand against the Illinois Standards Achievement Test (ISAT). Never a popular exam among parents, who did not like the pressure put on children to perform well, or among teachers, who did not receive results in time for the data to be useful in their instructional planning, this was the test that was used to determine whether elementary schools had made adequate yearly progress toward the 2014 mandate of 100% student proficiency in core academic subjects under No Child Left Behind (NCLB) legislation. That year's administration of the test was viewed as meaningless for several reasons: NCLB targets largely had been proven unrealistic; CPS had replaced several of the exam's other uses with different tests; and ISAT, not being aligned with the newly adopted Common Core State Standards, was set to be discarded the following year in favor of another instrument.

Politically savvy activist parents played a pivotal role in the rebellion against the 2014 ISAT. Local testing-resistance organization More Than a Score (MTAS) Chicago had long advocated for authentic approaches to assessment and alternatives to high-stakes testing. Its website (www.morethanascorechicago.org) makes available fact sheets, how-to kits, and sample letters that Chicago parents can use to keep their children out of some or all of the dozens of tests administered in CPS schools. In the run-up to the low-stakes 2014 ISAT, the group started a campaign to educate fellow city parents on their rights to direct the education of their children, and specifically to explain the procedures and consequences for not participating in ISAT testing.

While parents in Illinois do not have the same legal right to opt out of testing that families in other states enjoy, there is a process for test "refusals," ensuring that the absence of a student's score will not be held against the teacher or the school. The response to the campaign was overwhelming—MTAS clearly had tapped into a widespread sense of frustration among families over how much time their children were spending in school being tested and about how much pressure they were feeling to improve their scores. More than 1,500 students at about 80 schools across the city did not participate in that year's administration (Dudek, Schlikerman, & Esposito, 2014).

Resistance also came from teachers, many of whom had long been critical of the intensifying role and increasingly severe consequences of standardized testing. The united faculties of two Chicago elementary schools, Drummond and Saucedo, voted to boycott the ISAT. Individual teachers at dozens of other CPS schools refused to take part in their campus administrations and most often were permitted to supervise or instruct the students who were not taking the exam (Dudek et al., 2014). Once again educators and families were working side by side in the struggle, only to be brought even closer together by the Chicago Public Schools' punitive response to both. Teachers were threatened with revoked licensure, and children were removed from their classrooms by district investigators and interrogated about why they hadn't taken the test (Krauser, 2014). Hundreds of teachers, parents, and supporters (Gregory and Isabel among them) came together on March 10 for a rally outside a CPS network office to protest the retaliatory actions by the district.

Teacher and community solidarity is indeed a significant win as a result of the strike, one not found in the contract language. At the same time, the most important losses are similarly not found in the final agreement, and their trajectories can be traced far beyond the Chicago strike both in time and in space. The campaign to dismantle public schooling has been gathering momentum for over a decade, using diverse strategies and attacking on many fronts. A key target for the forces of privatization—likely because they are equaled in potential power only by public school parents—is the teaching profession and teachers themselves. At the same time that expectations of teachers have been intensifying, so has the public perception that teachers are failing.

The disparagement of teachers is not a new phenomenon in the United States. Even before the 20th century, the fictional Ichabod Crane, physically unattractive and ethically questionable, presented an unappealing public image of the American schoolmaster (Irving, 1893). His weaknesses—of body and spirit—have ready parallels in the cinematic representations of career educators, most of whom serve to obstruct the single "savior" teacher in movies like *Freedom Writers* (LaGravenese, 2007). Teachers have long served as scapegoats for various national crises, from the Russians winning the space race (Spring, 2011) to the earlier mentioned current security concerns (Klein & Rice, 2012). The latest attacks, however, have expanded beyond teacher competence to encompass our characters. No longer are teachers assumed to be in the profession because of a desire to do public service.

Discrediting teachers has been highly effective at keeping educators' voices out of the public debates on school policy. Classroom-derived knowledge and experience have been so devalued that superintendents—often referred to in the recent turn toward a corporate model as district CEOs—are being hired from fields completely unconnected to education. Even principals need no longer have spent any time in the schools, since the leadership academies of the Broad Foundation and others are "designed to recruit noneducator corporate, military and nonprofit leaders" (Saltman, 2010, p. 79) for these positions. Considering how thoroughly teachers have been painted as ineffective and even immoral, it should come as no surprise that, in today's climate, being a professional educator is the worst possible qualification for having a say in the way schools are run.

This is no accident. Silencing the voices that are most likely to guide us to the loftier visions we might nourish and build for education in this country serves the project of school privatization quite well. In recent decades, the messaging around education as workforce preparation alone—and around schools as failing in that mission since 1983's *A Nation at Risk* report (Spring, 2011)—has become nearly hegemonic, that is, agreed upon across the country, among individuals from all walks of life, and on both sides of the red–blue political divide. It is important to remember, however, that this is not the only way that we can think about the purpose of schools—or the only way that we ever have.

THE PURPOSES OF EDUCATION

Historically, there have been four broad philosophical approaches to conceptualizing the aims of education. In times past, proponents of one or another of these engaged in spirited public exchange with adherents of the others, and many educators and scholars debated internally and in their writing about which of these valuable perspectives should take priority at any given time or in any particular context. These conversations served to keep education democratic, to ensure that schools met the needs of diverse populations and constituents. As the conflicts have faded, so have the philosophical views left behind and, more important, so too have the possibilities to imagine schools in new and different ways.

The four philosophies are engagingly presented in an article by curriculum historian William H. Schubert (1996)—as well as in his teaching—where each perspective is personified and presented as a "guest speaker." The four philosophies, with the corresponding practitioners Schubert introduces, are: progressivism/ experientialist; perennialism/intellectual traditionalist; essentialism/social behaviorist; and reconstructionism/critical reconstructionist. Schubert terms the philosophies "curriculum traditions," and explores how advocates of each would respond to the basic curriculum "question of what is worth knowing" (p. 169). Each tradition also reflects more broadly a view of what schools are and what they should accomplish, as demonstrated below.

The philosophy represented by Schubert's (1996) experientialist, also referred to as progressivism (Oliva & Gordon, 2013; Ornstein, 2015), is best known through the work of John Dewey (1902), its most famous proponent and arguably the most influential educational philosopher in modern history. Unfortunately, and in spite of Dewey's prominence in the field, this perspective has had only a limited—and rapidly diminishing—influence on the experience of teachers and students in most classrooms. This approach begins with consideration of the individual student and would have schools nurture the growth and fulfillment of that unique being, largely by facilitating the learner's own process of discovery in self-selected areas of interest. Despite definitive evidence of the remarkable academic achievement of students educated in such a manner (Kridel & Bullough, 2007), schools have mostly ignored the experientialist perspective. Nearly the only place this philosophy holds sway is in the early childhood classroom, but even here it is under threat as testing and "accountability" expand their reach.

The approach of the intellectual traditionalist reflects the educational philosophy of perennialism (Oliva & Gordon, 2013; Ornstein, 2015). For this "speaker," the role of education is cultural preservation and transmission. In other words, schools should prepare students to be a part of a shared cultural community by providing the background knowledge necessary to understand aesthetic, literary, historical, scientific, numeric, and other forms of reference—as occurs in a rigorous program in the liberal arts. While some scholars whose work promotes this view, like E. D. Hirsch, Jr., who coined the term "cultural literacy" (1987), appear to have a Euro- and androcentric understanding of what constitutes the canon, Schubert's (1996) personified philosophy is open to a more inclusive version of our cultural heritage, incorporating the contributions of diverse peoples and thinkers. The intellectual traditionalist perspective, while not the most influential in this country, has not been wholly abandoned. The new Common Core State Standards can be seen as reflecting this understanding of the purpose of education.

The philosophy presented by Schubert's (1996) social behaviorist, termed essentialism elsewhere (Oliva & Gordon, 2013; Ornstein, 2015), prioritizes productivity, efficiency, and societal economic progress. In this view, schools should serve the very practical purpose of preparing students to become successful, contributing members of society. Successful contribution is to be defined empirically; the best means of facilitating such an outcome is to be derived scientifically; and progress toward these ends must be carefully measured and monitored. The theoretical contributions to psychology of B. F. Skinner (1976), generally referred to as behaviorism, were instrumental in the development of this tradition, which is ascendant in the current historical period in U.S. education—almost to the point of hegemony. This philosophy underlies our understanding of schooling as preparation for participation in the workforce, our view of pedagogy as all science and no art, and our reliance on standardized test scores as the measure of a successful education.

The philosophical stance of the critical reconstructionist (Schubert, 1996), sometimes simply called reconstructionism (Oliva & Gordon, 2013; Ornstein, 2015), holds that schools should be the catalysts for positive social change. In some contexts, this might mean empowering students to overcome societal oppression. In others, this may require enlightening students as to the existence of social injustices. In any school, this approach involves fostering a critical mindset, a readiness to ask challenging questions about conditions that adult society seems to take for granted. Arising during the widespread hardship and dramatic inequality of the Great Depression—an economic situation not unlike that being experienced by many today—this perspective was first articulated by George S. Counts (1932b), who broke away from Dewey and the Progressive Education Association by stating that "a movement honestly styling itself progressive should engage in the positive task of creating a new tradition in American life" (p. 262). While this philosophy is reflected in some structural aspects of education, notably the tenure system's protection of teachers' free speech, it has had the least influence on educational practice of all the historical traditions.

In order to reclaim the conversation on education policy, we first need to reignite the debate among educational philosophies. Somewhere along the way, a single approach—and a limited and limiting version of that tradition—became the default view of the purpose of education. We know how it happened in many institutions that prepare teachers. Coursework requirements and licensure examinations have proliferated, leaving departments, faculty, and students scrambling to keep up with an ever-more-onerous certification process. When programs needed to be cut, many, if not most, chose to sacrifice the least "practical" areas of study: the humanities and the foundations of education. In this way, many teachers entered the profession without a background in the history of education or the philosophy of education—sometimes without having studied any learning theory. The perceived necessities of regulatory compliance meant the loss of foundations coursework and with it a philosophical conversation among professional educators.

Ironically, it is a strong philosophical grounding that enables a successful educational enterprise, whether in an individual teacher's practice or in a school system. The American Educational Research Association is the 35,000-member professional organization with the widest reach and the strongest voice in the academic field of education. At its 2014 annual meeting, David L. Kirp (2013a) was the sole recipient of the Outstanding Book Award—the highest honor possible for a work of educational research—for his qualitative study of the remarkable transformation of the school system in Union City, New Jersey. The Union City Public Schools serve the kind of population we have come to expect will struggle academically. Demographically, the students are overwhelmingly poor and from Spanish-speaking homes. Many of their parents lack documentation. A couple of decades ago, the schools were about as successful as statistics have led us to expect—that is, failing dismally.

Today, Union City students lead the state in test scores, and, more important, 90% graduate and 75% go to college. What is most interesting, however, is that this amazing improvement has not come as the result of any of the reforms being sold as the panacea that will cure our ailing educational system. There were no turnarounds and no charter schools. Teachers were not fired en masse, and the district did not have a contract with Teach for America. As Kirp explained from the dais when accepting his award, the leadership of the Union City schools decided to start from the beginning, with developing a shared philosophy. In building this foundation, a true community emerged among administrators, teachers, students, and parents. United in purpose and working collaboratively, with a curriculum designed to achieve those ends, the city's schools slowly but steadily improved.

If it were not for Kirp's book, this kind of story would never have made the pages of *The New York Times* (Kirp, 2013b). There is no oomph, no near-vertical slope on the data chart. This is also not the kind of story that can be replicated and exported to struggling urban school systems across the country. A place-based, community-derived philosophy is by definition unique and context-specific. It won't work somewhere else. But what can be shared, and what can make a difference in other locations, is the impetus to conversation, to thinking and talking about what schools should be and do—and from there about what *our* schools *here* should be and do.

Most of us haven't thought about education in quite this way for a long time. It will take a shift in gears to a slower and more reflective pace. And, in this educational climate, it will take a fierce determination to defend the public interest in directing the work of our schools. Teachers have as a model the Chicago Teachers Union under the leadership of the CORE caucus. While their narrative can't be replicated any more than that of the Union City schools, the CTU during the teachers' strike of 2012 demonstrated what inclusive, democratic decisionmaking around education policy can look like. Let's see whether we can do the same in schools and systems around the country.

A Strike of Choices by Gregory Michie

So, Mayor Rahm Emanuel said the Chicago Teachers Union engaged in a "strike of choice." I'd say it was more like a strike of choices. After all, it's rare that anything is chosen in a vacuum. Choices are made within a context, a climate, and often in response to other choices made at an earlier time. To call what happened in Chicago a "strike of choice" is to deny how we got to that point, to conveniently ignore the prelude of choices that came before.

When Emanuel's appointed school board rescinded the 4% raises due to Chicago Public School teachers according to their contract, that was a choice. When the mayor promised a longer school day without knowing how he'd pay for it or consulting those most affected, that was a choice. When he pushed for a state law that would make it harder for Chicago teachers to strike, and require that teacher evaluations be based partly on student test scores, that was a choice. And, when he relentlessly praises charter schools, or backs unproven "reforms" that are widely seen by researchers and educators alike as harmful—those, too, are choices.

All this added up to create a tense, combustible atmosphere surrounding the city's schools. The mayor blamed teachers, but anybody who'd been paying even casual attention knew the deal. I'd been watching the situation pretty closely during the previous year in my role as a professor of education. But, thanks to a choice I made over the summer, I again had a front-row seat: I left my full-time university faculty position to return to teaching 7th- and 8th-graders at a Chicago Public School.

Of course, a lot had changed for teachers since I left CPS in 1999. I don't remember uttering the word *data* once during my previous 9-year tenure, but it's a data-driven world in schools now. Many would say that's a clear sign of how far teaching has come as a profession. Count me as a skeptic.

But some things are as I remember them. Many teachers still show up the week before their work year officially begins, spending entire days getting their rooms ready. Educators' supply stores are still full of teachers spending their own money, sometimes hundreds of dollars, on materials for their students and their classrooms. It's still common for teachers to stay at school well beyond the final bell, preparing for the next day, collaborating with colleagues, or counseling students. And even in the uncertainty surrounding the looming strike, when it would've been easy to be bitter or distracted, teachers—to a person, from what I saw—made the choice to remain upbeat and hopeful, to stay focused on the kids, the work at hand. "I have a feeling it's going to be a great year," one veteran teacher told me, and others seemed to echo that sentiment with the way they approached their days.

So, when Mayor Emanuel called the action by the Chicago Teachers Union a "strike of choice," and implied that teachers were choosing their own interests over those of their students, I took it personally. And when the *Chicago Tribune*'s editorial board wrote that the city's striking teachers "abandoned the children they say they're committed to teaching," I was incensed. Judging from the size of the downtown rallies, I was far from alone.

The mayor seemed to think public opinion was with him, but it was another sign that he was out of touch. The *Chicago Sun-Times* reported that a survey of 500 registered voters showed that 47% supported the teachers' strike, while 39% opposed it. Out in the neighborhoods, the car-horn vote was even more lopsided. Based on days of picketing with fellow teachers in the Back of the Yards neighborhood, I'd say the honks and hollers of support outnumbered the thumbs-down gestures about 500 to 1. And the encouragement came from a wide cross-section of Chicago's working and middle classes: Latinos, African Americans, Whites, Asians, parents, former students, Chicago Transit Authority drivers, police officers, landscapers, plumbers, streets and sanitation crews, roofers, long haulers, and people who drive tortilla trucks, milk trucks, and beer trucks, too. These may not be members of the Commercial Club of Chicago, but I bet most of them vote.

The real shows of solidarity, though, came in the downtown marches and rallies. The sea of red, the common purpose, the swelling pride in the important work teachers do, the reconnections with teacher-friends who work in far-flung corners of the city. One of my favorite moments was when a large circle of teachers and their supporters formed around a group of drummers and impromptu dancers, all of us bouncing up and down and chanting to the beat, "I believe we are gonna win! I believe we are gonna win!"

It's too easy, of course, to cast this strike, or any social conflict, in terms of good versus bad, winners and losers. But while it wasn't a strike of choice in the sense the mayor intended, it really was a strike about choices—about which direction we the people want public education to go. Do we want to keep heading down the same road of more testing, more data slicing, more reforms based on a business model? Or do we want our schools to aspire to something different, something better, something more?

In the midst of the strike, one of my new teaching colleagues, a first-year teacher who grew up in the neighborhood, brought her younger brother along to picket in front of a nearby school. He was 10 years old and in 5th grade. For several hours he stood among us rather unassuming, listening to the passing cars honk their approval, holding up a hand-lettered sign.

"I am in the middle of a lesson," it read.

Aren't we all.

The Sound of Solidarity by Isabel Nuñez

When we arrived at the green square of Union Park on September 15, we were greeted by the sounds of 18-wheelers, air horns blaring and trailers rumbling. At first we craned our necks looking for an accident, but we didn't see one. It was only after we'd walked down the el station steps that we found out what the commotion was. "Honk if you support Chicago teachers!" the signs called out, and it seemed that every truck, bus, taxi, and car going by wanted to add to the noise.

And there was more noise to come. After a week of being on strike, the Chicago Teachers Union had gathered tens of thousands of its members and supporters for a rally, and it was loud. I wandered around the park with Joe, my partner, and Maeve, my daughter, hearing impassioned voices over the loudspeaker and greeting friends and students in my graduate courses. Between fortuitous encounters and text messages, I found out that all of my colleagues from Concordia University Chicago's Center for Policy Studies and Social Justice—including the coauthors of this volume—were in the park as well.

Nearing the baseball diamond, we heard the beat of a drum line. The students of the Kelly High School marching band had showed up, in their street clothes, to support their teachers. The band was with us as we began to march west down Washington Boulevard, amid a sea of red T-shirts. We were surrounded by teachers, and with our 4-year-old marcher lifting her knees high, we soon lost sight of the band. That didn't mean we lacked for music, though. As we moved among the bobbing homemade placards, we kept time to the voices singing out the refrain, "This is what democracy looks like!"

The march was long, but we didn't notice. The teachers especially, having walked the picket lines throughout the week, must have been exhausted. But the last noise we remember echoed the first and did a lot to ease the fatigue. The street was lined for miles by supporters, chanting and cheering from windows and balconies. The people of Chicago were saluting us, making noise in support of their teachers. In those last steps of the march, we realized that we'd been carried on the shoulders of the city.

The Reluctant Boycotter by Gregory Michie

When I returned to a Chicago Public School classroom in 2012 after a decade as a university professor, I thought I understood the scope of the testing frenzy. I'd spent time in dozens of Chicago school buildings observing student teachers, and I'd seen the testing push grow more and more intense. But being in a school all day, every day, gave me a new perspective.

The color-coded CPS Assessment Calendar designated 23 weeks of the school year as testing windows of one kind or another. My 8th-graders were slated to take the NWEA/MAP test (three times), as well as the ISAT, the EXPLORE, the NAEP, district-mandated REACH performance tasks (twice), and, for English language learners, the ACCESS. Even kindergartners and 1st-graders weren't exempt: They would have to sit through two 40-question "computer-adaptive" exams. It was no coincidence, I thought, that the verb administer is used to accompany both harsh punishments and standardized tests.

Because CPS used both the NWEA/MAP and the ISAT to make high-stakes decisions about student promotion and "school quality," they caused particular anxiety for students and teachers. So when the district announced that the Spring 2014 administration of the ISAT would be its last—and would have no high stakes attached to it—teachers welcomed the news. The relief was fleeting, though, as the ISAT was being bumped in favor of soon-to-come, Common Core–aligned, "next-generation" assessments.

With no stakes attached to the lame-duck ISAT, a coalition of parent and community groups called More Than a Score Chicago began urging parents to sign letters opting their children out of the test. Around the city, hundreds of parents did so. Many seemed to view the opt-out movement not only as a statement against the ISAT, but as a revolt against the entire top-down, market-based, test-driven direction CPS schools had taken over the preceding decade.

As momentum continued to build just a week before the ISAT was scheduled to begin, a group of teachers from Saucedo Scholastic Academy raised the stakes even higher. They held a press conference announcing that they planned to boycott the ISAT. News reports said as many as two dozen teachers at the school had agreed not to give the test, and hundreds of Saucedo students intended to opt out as well. CPS responded by threatening disciplinary action—including possible revocation of state teaching licenses—but the Saucedo teachers didn't budge. A few days later, as an exclamation point, teachers at another CPS school, Drummond, said they would join the boycott.

Watching all this unfold, I felt like a phony. For years I'd spoken out against the abuses of high-stakes tests. I'd written op-eds. I'd given talks and appeared on panels. I'd encouraged prospective teachers I'd taught to find ways to resist the pressure of teaching to the test once they had classrooms of their own. But here I was, standing on the sidelines as other teachers put their jobs on the line. It didn't feel right.

I knew, as the Saucedo and Drummond organizers obviously did, that there was strength in numbers. But I doubted we could convince even a small group of teachers at my school to join the boycott. Our situation was precarious in that our school had been placed on probation earlier in the year. Folks were already worried about losing their jobs. Tension in the building was high. I thought briefly about going out on a limb by myself, but that seemed too risky: I'd given up a tenure-track university position to return to CPS as a nontenured teacher. So, with gritted teeth, I walked into my classroom the following Monday morning with a box of ISAT test booklets under my arm.

That's when I learned that, over the weekend, our school's list of more than 40 students whose parents had signed opt-out letters had somehow been whittled down to fewer than 10. And it wasn't only at our school. A colleague across the hall heard via email that parents at schools throughout the south and west sides had received phone calls "strongly encouraging" them not to opt their children out. Some students said their parents were told that the school would lose funding if their child didn't take the test. Others said they were told that the school could forfeit teaching positions.

I was furious. Tactics like those would never even be attempted with middle-class parents, I thought. But like CPS's repeated threats against boycotting teachers, this had little to do with the ISAT. State law or not, that test was as good as buried. What district leaders were trying desperately to protect was the edifice of corporate-style school reform. Testing was the base that the entire house of cards rested on, and if boycotts and opt-outs were allowed to succeed on a wide scale, the whole deck could come tumbling down.

But I didn't have the luxury of focusing on that for long. Moments later, a woman walked into my room and informed me she'd been sent to proctor my test session. Upper grade classrooms almost never had proctors in our school, so the reason for her presence seemed clear: I was being monitored. I walked down the hall to confirm my suspicions, and sure enough: Two other teachers on my team who'd also been vocal about the opt-out movement had been assigned proctors as well. Soon thereafter, I got a two-word text from one of them, who had walked off in protest. "I'm out," it said.

As the appointed time for the test approached, I stood by the intercom button, steaming. Should I walk out, too? Should I cool off and think things over tonight? I knew my 7th-graders could tell something was wrong, that I was agitated, angry. I felt bad that I might be making them uneasy when the assessment was about to begin, but the truth was it didn't really matter how they did.

"Break the seal on your test booklets and turn to page 2," I said, checking the clock. They all did as they were told.

The next morning, I came in and told my principal that I couldn't, in good conscience, give the test for the rest of the week. I also told my homeroom students, saying that I hoped they understood that I was standing up for what I thought was right, and that I wouldn't do anything that I thought would have negative repercussions for them or the school.

"What's gonna happen to you?" one asked.

"I don't know," I said. "I guess we'll see."

I sent an email to all the teachers at my school, explaining why I'd decided to boycott and emphasizing that it wasn't a decision I had made lightly or recklessly. Other than a couple of close friends on my teaching team, only three colleagues responded. In the halls, I felt a chilly reception from co-workers who normally would at least say hello. They were worried, I figured, that my protest somehow would end up hurting our chances of getting off probation. But beyond that, the lack of support I felt reminded me of the palpable sense of fear that permeates so many school buildings in the age of test-and-punish reform. "Everybody's afraid," a CPS teacher-friend once told me. "Until we get over that fear, it's going to be hard to make a change."

Eventually, things cooled down and the heightened tension of the moment relaxed. The hammer of punishment from

CPS never dropped—as least it hasn't as I write this—and the end of the year came, bittersweet as always. A thank-you card I got from one graduating 8th-grader provided a fitting bookend to the whole experience: "Thanks for helping me do so good on my reading on the MAP test," he wrote. "Even though you hate it."

SUGGESTED READING LIST

Bruno, R., Ashby, S., & Manzo, F. (2012). *Beyond the classroom: An analysis of a Chicago public school teacher's actual workday*. Urbana, IL: Labor Education Program, University of Illinois at Urbana-Champaign. Available at www.ler.illinois.edu/labor/images/Teachers%20Activity-Time%20Study%202012%20(1)-Final.pdf

This is the report of a study on teachers' time use in the city of Chicago. Survey data collected from 983 teachers show an average work week of 58 hours, with 9 hours daily spent at school and several hours more working at home, including on weekends.

Carl, J. C. (2009). "Good politics is good government": The troubling history of mayoral control of the public schools in twentieth-century Chicago. *American Journal of Education, 115*(2), 305–336.

This history of school governance in Chicago posits that the strong elected executives in the city have long directed the workings of the school system, making it a valuable test case for the recent trend toward mayoral control in urban education.

CReATE. (2012). *Misconceptions and realities about teacher and principal evaluation*. Chicago, IL: Author. Available at http://www.createchicago.org/2012/03/misconceptions-and-realities-about.html

This is a letter written by Chicago-area academics detailing the lack of a basis in research for using student test scores for teacher evaluation. Publicly presented to the Chicago mayor, schools CEO, and board of education, it warns against overreliance on such measures.

Designs for Change. (2012). *Chicago's democratically-led elementary schools far out-perform Chicago's turnaround schools*. Chicago, IL:

Author. Available at www.designsforchange.org/democracy_vs_turnarounds.pdf

This report on the comparative achievement outcomes for different types of schools in Chicago calls into question the touted benefits of school turnarounds. Elementary schools governed by local school councils demonstrated much stronger results than campuses so "reformed."

Labor Notes. (2014). *How to jump-start your union: Lessons from the Chicago teachers*. Detroit, MI: Author.

This book presents the social organizing done by the CORE caucus of the Chicago Teachers Union as a model for the rejuvenation of labor groups around the country, presenting in detail the efforts and strategies that led to the success of the 2012 strike.

Lipman, P., & Gutstein, E. (2013). The rebirth of the Chicago Teachers Union and possibilities for counter-hegemonic education movement. *Monthly Review, 65*(2), 1–12.

This article contextualizes the 2012 Chicago teachers' strike within the city's recent education history. Chicago's schools have been the targets of aggressive neoliberal policy reforms, and the authors present the strike as an important demonstration of the possibilities for resistance.

Noonan, S., Farmer, S., & Huckaby, F. (2014). *A sea of red: Chicago Teachers Union members reflect on how the social organizing model of unionism helped win the union's 2012 contract campaign*. Chicago, IL: Chicago Teachers Union. Available at www.ctunet.com/quest-center/research/text/A-SEA-OF-RED-February-2014.pdf

This report, published by the Chicago Teachers Union, presents the results of a qualitative study by outside researchers on members' experiences of the 2012 strike. Based on interviews with 37 individuals, the report illustrates the potential for unions as centers of social movement building.

Saltman, K. J. (2010). *The gift of education: Public education and venture philanthropy*. New York, NY: Palgrave Macmillan.

This book, published 2 years before the Chicago teachers' strike, provides background on the neoliberal education policies that the union was resisting. The work traces the origins of recent reforms to philanthropy from individuals whose business interests stand to profit from them.

Schubert, W. H. (1996, Summer). Perspectives on four curriculum traditions. *Educational Horizons, 74*(4), 169–176.

This journal article presents, in an accessible format, the four ways of understanding the purpose of education. Each perspective is personified as one of several speakers: intellectual traditionalist, social behaviorist, experientialist, and critical reconstructionist.

Uetricht, M. (2014). *Strike for America: Chicago teachers against austerity.* Brooklyn, NY: Verso.

This book, written by a local journalist, examines the history of the CORE caucus of the CTU, how it earned leadership of the union, and how it led Chicago teachers in a successful strike for a fair contract.

Students, Teachers, and Schools

A few years ago, Jonathan Kozol spoke on the University of Chicago campus. Several of us made it a fieldtrip for our master's courses, staking out a few rows toward the middle of the lefthand side where our graduate students could sit and hear the writer of some of the most influential volumes on education of recent decades. Even if the students (all practicing teachers) hadn't read any of *Savage Inequalities* (1992), they had at least heard of it. We learned a lot from his address: about schools but also about Kozol himself. In a generally impassioned speech, he showed the strongest emotions when recalling his testimony on student/teacher ratios before a group of legislators. As Kozol described his rage at the lawmakers' dismissal of the benefits of smaller class sizes, his previously mainstream-sounding dialect became more and more posh—very much that of a Boston Brahmin.

In times of great emotion, multilingual and multidialectal individuals often return to their native language, which is usually the one that holds the most meaning for them. Googling Kozol back at the office, we discovered that he was indeed from Boston and had graduated from exactly the kind of prestigious prep school that the legislators' own children likely attended, certain to boast very small class sizes. No wonder he was so angry—he knew from experience what a small class size makes possible.

All the authors of this book have taught in public K–12 classrooms. Each of us also knows from experience what a difference every increment in class size makes to what we as teachers are able to accomplish with our students. For Pamela's and Gregory's radio and media students, the math is pretty straightforward. Every additional student meant that each of the others had less "air time." Isabel was teaching in California before and after the passage of that state's 1996 class-size-reduction law. While some experts argue that the policy was implemented too rapidly to benefit the highest-need students and schools (Jepsen & Rivkin, 2002), she well remembers the additional physical, emotional, and intellectual space in her 1st-grade classroom when 34 desks became 20.

The strongest research to date on the effects of smaller class sizes on student achievement was undertaken by the state of Tennessee beginning in 1985 (Mosteller, 1995). Project STAR (Student/Teacher Achievement Ratio) sought to determine the short- and long-term impact of smaller classes in kindergarten through 3rd grade. The controlled experiment involved the random assignment of thousands of students in hundreds of classrooms at dozens of schools in groups of 13–17, 22–25 with a paraprofessional, or 22–25 without an aide. The initial phase of the study showed substantial cognitive and academic benefits for students in the smaller classes (about 10 percentile points) and about a third of this for students with a classroom aide. Notably, initial gains for minority students in the smaller classes were double those for nonminority students (Nye, Hedges, & Konstantopoulos, 2000). The second phase of the research showed that the benefits of class-size reductions in the early years persisted long after students entered later grades with higher class sizes (Krueger & Whitmore, 2001).

As a large urban school district with perennial budget woes, the Chicago Public School district has its share of overcrowded classrooms. Class-size guidelines are significantly above even the "large" classes in the Tennessee experiment (28–31 students, as opposed to 22–25) and are regularly exceeded—some by as much as 50% (Lutton, 2013). Chicago's teachers have the clearest view of the harm done to children by being taught in such large groups, which is why the Chicago Teachers Union included smaller class sizes as one of its demands during the Fall 2012 strike. Despite the legal proscription from striking over concerns about students, the teachers brought this student-focused demand to the table anyway, usefully reversing their guiding mantra to assert that "students' learning conditions are teachers' working conditions."

For many of Chicago's striking teachers, this was a bit of an extrapolation from what was really motivating the class-size demand. Student learning, at least as measured in the Project STAR study, was determined by test scores. While any teacher would be pleased by students' strong performance on an exam, for many this is not the final judgment of success or the primary objective. For these teachers, the benefits of having fewer students in the room can't be captured in statistical effect sizes—and perhaps not even through qualitative interviews. Some educators believe their most important work in the classroom is not academic, but more broadly developmental. They appreciate smaller class sizes because they allow for deeper relationships between teachers and individual students, and among the student members of the classroom community.

Closer connections in the classroom mean more individualized guidance and stronger support networks, beneficial to academic learning certainly but not exclusively. When a teacher knows students deeply—their talents and struggles, what motivates and what frightens them—that teacher is better able to nurture growth in every area of life, to help the individual become not just a better student but a better person. When a whole classroom of students know one another well enough to laugh and cry together, to agree emphatically on some things and disagree just as vehemently about others, the room can become a microcosm of a beautifully functioning democracy, where every voice is raised and every opinion is valued. On the national level, we are dishearteningly far from this ideal at the moment, but perhaps a return to one of our historical purposes for education would allow a future generation of leaders to bring us closer to it.

SCHOOLING FOR DEMOCRACY

The acknowledged intellectual architect of our common system of public schooling, Horace Mann, was motivated by a perceived threat to democracy in the form of growing ethnic diversity and wealth stratification in the United States of the mid-19th century (Spring, 2013). The common school as then envisioned was a force of cultural assimilation, designed to strengthen the appeal of the vote as an alternative to social unrest, but the original impetus was to enhance the democratic process.

Many other influential figures in the history of American education have shared central aspects of this view. Most significant of these is John Dewey, the educational philosopher who is still so revered as to be cited ubiquitously in the literature of the field (just as we are doing here!). Dewey (1922) echoed his predecessor, but was less motivated by fear. Instead of molding diverse students into a common culture, he looked to facilitate communication across disparate groups.

> The devotion of democracy to education is a familiar fact. . . . A democracy is more than a form of government; it is primarily a mode of associated living, of conjoint communicated experience. The extension in space of the number of individuals who participate in an interest so that each has to refer his own action to that of others, and to consider the action of others to give point and direction to his own, is equivalent to the breaking down of those barriers of class, race, and national territory which kept men from perceiving the full import of their activity. (p. 101)

His words describe an ideal classroom community, where every member is invested in the good of the whole. Such a group dynamic is fostered more easily with the student/teacher ratios recommended by Project STAR and accomplishes more when the student population reflects a broader range of our diversity.

According to this philosophical approach to schooling, every individual in the classroom is of incalculable value to society, with a unique and unforeseeable contribution to make. For this reason, each student deserves to be nurtured in developing most fully into the best person he or she can be. This perspective, which Schubert (1996) calls experientialism and others call progressivism (Oliva & Gordon, 2013; Ornstein, 2015), is still guided by Deweyan educational philosophy, but is difficult to discern in the current public school landscape outside of early childhood classrooms.

Experientialist pedagogies, with their emphasis on individual students' self-guided discovery and real-world relevance, are challenging to implement in an age of standardization and narrow accountability. The demands of teaching to high-stakes tests narrow the classroom curriculum, squeezing out the cultural connections to diverse student groups that many teachers work to bring into their instruction. The practical experience of interacting with diverse groups of students in integrated learning groups—preparation for active participation in a vibrant political democracy—is disappearing as schools become more segregated. Even the democratic benefits of learning from teachers with a variety of life experiences and worldviews are becoming rarer as the teaching force itself grows Whiter and more limited to individuals with middle-class backgrounds.

CULTURALLY AND LINGUISTICALLY DIVERSE LEARNERS

Of course, we don't often hear about democracy as the goal of our schools these days. Politicians and principals alike are much more likely to point to global economic competitiveness as the purpose of education. If this is truly the aim of our educational system in the United States, then we are lucky indeed. As a nation of immigrants that is still a highly desired destination among countless individuals and families around the world, we are extraordinarily well resourced for the global economy in terms of languages spoken and cultural competence. With only 52% of our public school population being White and non-Hispanic (Wells, 2014), there is a great deal of diversity in U.S. classrooms.

Every culturally and linguistically diverse student in our schools has knowledge and understandings that can help to develop the products, marketing approaches, and relationships that are essential to successfully doing business in their countries of origin. Their diversity also can enrich with new perspectives the public conversation about the good life and the good society. We should be strengthening these resources through strong bilingual and bicultural education programs, so that these students can make the greatest possible future contribution. Somehow, we are not doing that. In fact, what is happening is just the opposite. We appear to be going out of our way to destroy the very cultural and linguistic resources that could strengthen our market share—and, more important, our democracy.

In this regard, each of us feels lucky to live in Illinois, where state policies for language-minority education are strong, even if local school practice doesn't always meet these high standards. Here, legislation establishes bilingual education as a state priority (Illinois School Code, 2010). Districts are required to provide instruction in students' native language when a school has 20 or more learners in the same language group; if there are 19 or fewer, there must be an English as a Second Language (ESL) program. A required component of both programs is "instruction in the history and culture of the country, territory, or geographic area that is the native land of the students or of their parents and in the history and culture of the United States" (Illinois Administrative Code, 2013).

Unfortunately, the nation as a whole does not have as enlightened a perspective on the preservation of immigrant languages. While there is no official U.S. language or language policy, languages decline here so precipitously that one of our colleagues in ESL refers to this country as "the place languages go to die." In stark contrast to the European Union, with its 23 official languages and advocacy of the "mother tongue plus two foreign languages" (Gándara et al., 2010, p. 20) for every one of its citizens, the United States remains a stubbornly monolingual society, even in an increasingly globalized world. The endangerment of English is demonstrably a myth: Native languages usually are lost within three generations, and the transition to English takes place in two or less "among all immigrant groups, including Spanish speakers, who are most often stigmatized as resistant to English" (Crawford, 2000, p. 6).

Despite the evidence that the English language is in no danger in the United States, several states have gone to extraordinary lengths to protect it. Some of these, like English-only laws, target the use of other languages in government communications (Crawford, 2000), while others address the threat to English posed by multilingual schoolchildren. In three states—California, Arizona, and Massachusetts—ballot initiatives have made it a crime to instruct students in a language other than English (Gándara & Hopkins, 2010).

The 1998 passage of California's Proposition 227 resulted in the percentage of English language learners (ELLs) being instructed in their native language dropping from 29.1% to 5.6% in less than 10 years (Wentworth, Pellegrin, Thompson, & Hakuta, 2010). The few remaining are most likely to be found in dual-language immersion programs, where ELLs and native English speakers are educated together in both groups' native languages, so that both graduate fully bilingual and biliterate. Clearly there is some recognition of the value of multilingualism in that state, since bilingual instruction remains legal when non-immigrant students are benefitting.

In 2000, voters in Arizona passed Proposition 203, which mandates Structured English Immersion for language learners and outlaws bilingual education. As a result, the proportion of English learners receiving native-language instruction declined from 32% in 1997 to 5% in 2004 (Mahoney, McSwan, Haladyna, & García, 2010). Interestingly, Massachusetts was, in 1971, the first state to mandate transitional bilingual education for its English learners. In 2002, it reversed course and became the third state to forbid such services when Referendum Question 2 went before the voters. While English learners, at 5.2%, are only a small proportion of the state's total student population, they number 29% of students in the Boston public schools (Uriarte, Tung, Lavan, & Diez, 2010).

It is only in the latter state that there was a noticeable change in academic outcomes in the years following the shift in policy, and it was overwhelmingly negative in the city of Boston, with achievement gaps widening and dropout rates increasing. Results in California and Arizona have been mixed. However, a broader view shows such policies to be harmful even to the short-term goals of improving ELL performance. Researchers (Rumberger & Tran, 2010) used National Assessment of Educational Progress (NAEP) scores to examine the achievement gaps between English-learner and English-proficient students across states with varying policies and practices. Fourth-grade reading and math scores were compared. In 4th grade, achievement gaps were bigger in states with the most restrictive language policies, and smaller in those states with the highest proportion of English learners receiving native-language instruction. While state policies did not seem to strongly affect overall achievement, they did have a great deal of influence on achievement gaps between language groups. Restrictive state language policies quite clearly correlate to larger gaps.

These outcomes aren't likely to surprise people who are familiar with second-language acquisition theory. The research in this area has long been clear that strengthening a learner's first language enhances learning in the second language (McGroarty, 1988). Recently, scholars have discovered new evidence that bilingualism confers generalized cognitive benefits that extend to every area of life—and even extend cognitive life itself. Studies have found that the onset of dementia, regardless of the underlying cause of the mental decline, occurs on average 5 years later for bilingual individuals toward the end of life (Bialystok, Craik, & Freedman, 2007; Craik, Bialystok, & Freedman, 2010). Considering our societal concerns with rising medical costs and an aging population, education policy should strive for universal bilingualism, not eradication of the linguistic resources we already possess.

Thankfully, parents, teachers, and other concerned citizens can have a large-scale beneficial impact on resistance to state-level policies that do not serve positive educational purposes. In California, the passage of Proposition 227 inspired just such a group to found an organization called Californians Together, which developed a statewide award called the California Seal of Biliteracy. Legislation in 2011 officially established the award, and the seal is affixed to the high school diploma of graduates in 165 California districts who have attained high levels of proficiency in at least two languages. The idea has spread to other states, and in 2014 Illinois lawmakers created an Illinois Seal of Biliteracy to mark the accomplishments of our own bilingual graduates.

Immigrant languages are not the only resource newcomers bring to our schools. Our culturally diverse student population embodies a wealth of understandings about the nations and societies from which their families emigrated. A commitment to validating and celebrating these backgrounds through multicultural education would be a wise approach to strengthening this resource. While this is certainly happening in some places, whether it is seen in policies like that of Illinois or in individual teachers' classroom practice, there is much working against multiculturalism in education. Arizona, for example, not only has outlawed bilingual education, but also has banned ethnic studies, rejecting a rich trove of indigenous knowledge about Latin American culture. Increasingly standardized curricula, controlled from above by administrators, leave teachers little room to integrate the cultures of the diverse students in their classrooms. If our shared goal is truly for schools to strengthen our nation's international economic competitiveness, it is difficult to discern the logic behind these policies. For those who look to our schools to make our democracy more vibrant, the policies seem even more misguided.

SCHOOL INTEGRATION

Looking closely at much of U.S. education policy with regard to culturally and linguistically diverse students, we do not appear to share a widespread commitment to education for democracy. Not only are we limiting these students' individual potential contributions, but we are restricting what they can offer to their peers in the area of embracing and learning from difference. We are 60 years beyond *Brown v. Board of Education* (1954), and our schools have not yet been integrated. In fact, we appear to be moving away from the vision enshrined in that landmark ruling as education policies intensify race- and class-based segregation in our nation's neighborhoods and schools (Orfield & Eaton, 1997).

Like many other challenges in education policy, segregation is not something that begins in the schools. For a long time our schools were segregated because our communities were segregated. It is also important to remember that housing segregation was neither accidental nor the simple result of innocent individual choices to live near others who are like us. Neighborhood segregation was state-sponsored and promoted by specific public policy choices, including "local zoning laws, racial segregation in public housing, and the purposeful exclusion of African-Americans from federal mortgage lending programs" (Wells, 2014, p. 9). Our history in Chicago with regard to this issue is particularly egregious, as the strategies used here to control the "threat" posed by the 1940s northward migration of Southern Blacks became a model for other cities and were even incorporated into federal legislation (Hirsch, 1998). Still, some progress in integrating schools did occur following the high court's ruling in *Brown*.

One very direct way that we are relinquishing the vision of *Brown* is by freeing districts of the regulatory legacy by abolishing judicial consent decrees. In the decades following the high court ruling, individuals in segregated districts sought relief through the legal system. Many cases resulted in consent decrees: voluntary agreements between plaintiffs and defendants to desegregate. In these cases, the decrees included detailed plans for integrating district schools with judicial oversight. In recent years, many districts have been released from their obligations under the consent decrees, even though schools are still substantially segregated. Unsurprisingly, segregation is intensifying as a result. In 1972, 18 years after *Brown*, 25% of Black students in the American South attended highly segregated schools; in Southern districts whose consent decrees were abolished between 1990 and 2011, 53% of Black students currently are attending such schools (Hannah-Jones, 2014).

The South wasn't the only part of the country that required court-ordered desegregation. The Chicago Public Schools' (2013b) own consent decree was issued in 1980, but was rescinded in 2009. However, in 2012, 179 schools in the district were over 90% Black, with over 90% of students eligible for free or reduced lunch (Caref, Hainds, Hilgendorf, Jankov, & Russell, 2012). Almost 40 years after the filing of their desegregation lawsuit in 1974, private plaintiffs in Tucson, Arizona, just had their desegregation order approved in February 2013 (U.S. Department of Justice, 2013). Clearly, the regulatory work of integrating our schools is not yet complete.

Resegregation did not begin with the disappearance of judicial consent decrees. Multiracial student populations at many schools still experienced separate and disparate educations through tracking, which divides students into different classes based on their academic abilities. Experience has shown that such tracks are highly racially segregating in otherwise integrated schools. Minority students in mixed-race tracked schools are more likely to be in the low tracks, even when their test scores and grades are stronger than those of their White peers in upper-level classes (Wells & Serna, 1996). This is referred to as second-generation segregation. It is measurably destructive to non-White students' academic achievement and self-esteem.

In those schools, at least there is a chance for students to interact with diverse peers in the cafeteria or through extracurricular activities. Other seemingly "colorblind" policy innovations have served to separate different populations of students more emphatically—at wholly different schools and even in wholly different communities (Wells, 2014). Several of these can be grouped under the umbrella of school choice. It seems that when families are allowed to choose, most choose segregated schools. In Milwaukee, so many White parents have opted for private-school vouchers that the city's public schools have been largely abandoned by them; the students are now almost entirely minority (Miner, 2013)

The national proliferation of charter schools also has served to intensify the race- and class-based segregation of our student population. According to enrollment data from 968 charter schools, these campuses are more racially segregated than the neighborhood schools in their districts and they further stratify students by class, with over 70% of these schools serving either mostly high-income or mostly low-income populations (Miron, Urschel,

Mathis, & Tornquist, 2010). The same study found that charter schools enroll fewer English language learners and students with special needs than do neighborhood schools. However, this may be changing, as a May 2014 longitudinal study of Chicago charters found special education enrollments to be slowly approaching parity with neighborhood schools. The researchers did find, however, that charters enrolled far fewer students with resource-intensive needs (Waitoller, Radinsky, Trzaska, & Maggin, 2014).

The determined "colorblindness" of our education policies seems to be motivated in part by a desire to leave behind a painful societal history with race and also to assuage resentment over perceived racial preference. As Chief Justice John Roberts famously wrote in his majority opinion overturning two cities' voluntary desegregation plans in *Parents Involved in Community Schools v. Seattle*, "The way to stop discrimination on the basis of race is to stop discriminating on the basis of race" (Wells, 2014, p. 5). However, a close look at the real impact of now-disfavored policies like affirmative action show that they have a profoundly positive effect for improving diversity, but an almost negligible effect on any individual White person's chances. A statistical rebuttal to the widespread criticisms of affirmative action first points out that Allan Bakke, the successful plaintiff in the case striking down the affirmative action policy at the University of California at Berkeley, actually had stronger test scores and a higher GPA than the majority of regular admissions—he was turned down for other reasons. But, even if he had been a genuine contender for a slot, the quota system worsened his odds only slightly (0.5% at the initial application stage, and 3% at the interview stage) (Liu, 2012, p. 245). When admissions are this selective, affirmative action makes very little difference to a particular White applicant's chances.

Nevertheless, such policies are disappearing in favor of the racially "neutral" policies that have the practical effect of solidifying the segregating impacts of racial dynamics in our far-from-colorblind society. Our children have fewer opportunities than we did to interact and develop relationships with peers who are not like them. Unless we can remedy this, they likely will grow up less adept at negotiating cultural difference, and less prepared to be successful in an economy that extends far beyond community, or even national, boundaries. More important, they may be less able to engage with diverse others in conversations about what we, as a people, want from our government. It may be harder to recognize that we are indeed one people united in a democratic system. Considering the stark divides in today's body politic, we may already be seeing the consequences of failing the vision of *Brown*.

DIVERSITY OF THE TEACHING FORCE

Chicago's teaching force looks different today than it did a decade or so ago. In 2000, the children of Chicago's city schools were nearly as likely to have an African American teacher as a White teacher; these odds were somewhat fair considering that just over half of CPS students that year were Black (Vevea, 2011). By 2011–2012, the city's 4 out of 10 African American students had only a 1-in-4 chance of learning from a teacher who looked like them (Chicago Public Schools, 2013a). School actions have had a starkly disproportionate effect on these odds; 65% of the teachers in closed schools were Black, as were 40% of tenured teachers who were laid off (Caref et al., 2012). Chicago's Latino children have never stood a good chance at having a teacher who shared their culture (11% of teachers for 34% of students in 2000), but the jobs lost to veteran Black teachers by and large did not go to Hispanics (18% of teachers for 44% of students in 2011–2012). The Consortium on Chicago School Research, which works out of the University of Chicago and is perhaps the most respected voice of educational research in the city, reported that the district's many recent school closings and turnarounds have resulted in a significantly Whiter, younger, and less experienced teaching corps (de la Torre et al., 2012)—and this in a report released before the record-setting closure of 50 mostly Black CPS schools in the summer of 2013.

If this is not enough, state-level policy decisions also have contributed to a less diverse teaching force in Illinois overall. In 2010, the score required to pass the basic skills portion of the state licensure exam was raised dramatically, and the rate of candidates passing fell from about 80% to about a third (Sawchuck, 2012). Minority candidates, who are less likely to possess the culturally specific background knowledge that standardized tests assume, particularly have struggled to reach the new minimums (only 18% pass). The result has been fewer teachers of color entering the classroom. The effect has been so concerning that in 2014 Illinois abandoned a policy that had accompanied the higher cut score: a limit on the number of times a candidate was allowed to take the test (Sanchez, 2014). While this is good news, as the doors to the profession will no longer be barred for prospective teachers who struggle on standardized exams, it does mean that the process of certification will become more expensive. Every time a candidate sits for the exam, it costs money.

The cost of professional preparation has long been an issue that affects the diversity of the teaching force. The price of a college education has been rising dramatically, while government support (such as Pell Grants) for poor and working-class students has been declining. Student teaching, which requires candidates to pay tuition while spending the whole of the work week as apprentices to their craft, can be an insurmountable challenge for prospective teachers whose families depend on their full-time wages. A new test of teaching proficiency, mandatory for teacher candidates in Illinois as of September 2015, will cost $300—if the candidate passes the first time around.

An examination of teacher preparation policy does shed some light on the teacher workforce demographic. The percentage of White teachers remains stubbornly above 80% (National Center for Education Statistics, 2013b), while the proportion of White students has declined to half—and very soon will be less than half (National Center for Education Statistics, 2013a). The percentage of our student population that are English learners is increasing, as well as spreading from the traditional destination states for immigrants, requiring more U.S. teachers to possess the specialized skills needed to teach them well (García, Arias, Harris Murri, & Serna, 2009). We are not suggesting that minority students need to be taught exclusively by minority teachers, but we do think that some of their teachers should be non-White. We also believe that White students should have some teachers who are from racial backgrounds different from their own. Experience with a diverse array of teachers—like experience with a diverse array of classmates—is the best way to prepare for a life lived with diverse others in a shared society.

Unfortunately, a review of recent studies (Achinstein, Ogawa, Sexton, & Freitas, 2010) found that, even when minority teachers are able to overcome policy obstacles like those in Illinois, there is a greater rate of job dissatisfaction and higher turnover among teachers of color (around 20%, as opposed to around 16% for White teachers). Interestingly, despite these overall trends, minority teachers are more likely than their White counterparts to work—and remain—in the high-need urban schools that are most difficult to staff. The researchers saw particular potential for retaining teachers of color in their humanistic motivations, school-level multicultural capital, and innovative, justice-oriented teacher education programs.

While retention of teachers of color is especially important given the demographic mismatch between the educator and student populations, we should be working toward policies that will improve retention of all teachers. Most hopefully in this regard, the greatest factor in teacher retention overall (more important than either teacher or student characteristics) is how teachers rate their schools' conditions, particularly "financial, human, and social capital" (Achinstein et al., 2010, p. 78). All of these can be manipulated through carefully considered local policy decisions. While the first two might require some investment of resources in the form of salaries and professional development opportunities, the latter could be improved with changes to scheduling that would allow more opportunity for teacher collaboration.

Teachers of all backgrounds can be successful educators of diverse students (Lowenstein, 2009), and all students should have teachers with a variety of personal characteristics and backgrounds. Because the proportion of teachers of color (less than 20%) is still so limited compared with White teachers, there remains important policy work to do in moving toward a more diverse teaching force (Hodgkinson, 2002).

RECLAIMING AN INCLUSIVE VISION

Successful advocacy for an integrated, multicultural educational experience for all is still possible. There have been recent setbacks to school desegregation by the U.S. Supreme Court, but those cases did not present central arguments related to the educational benefits of diversity—and in prior cases the justices have looked favorably on such reasoning (Wells, 2014). From our own experiences in the classroom (K–12 and collegiate), each of us would testify to the rich possibilities for teaching and learning that are opened by a culturally and linguistically diverse student body—and faculty. The more we have to learn from one another's lives and backgrounds, the more every person in the class gains. However, the benefits are not limited to those that accrue to the individual.

The whole of our society gains when diverse teachers and students learn together. The world is a multicultural place, and if students are to grow up and engage that world successfully, they need to gain experience with diversity as part of their school experience. If our aim is to develop a citizenry that will interact cooperatively with the world and a workforce that will compete effectively in a global economic market, educational efforts toward multilingualism and multiculturalism are a must. Integrated and diverse schools better prepare students for life in a democratic and multicultural nation. In these classrooms, students learn to listen to others who are not like themselves, and to express their own views effectively to different kinds of people. Students in such schools learn first-hand about other life experiences and the diverse worldviews and perspectives that result from them. Knowing about difference will make our students stronger and more engaged democratic citizens.

Race Traitor by Pamela Konkol

I remember the first time I was called a "race traitor" by a class full of graduate students. It wasn't fun.

As an educator of educators who teaches graduate-level courses in the social and philosophical foundations, having emotionally charged discussions about the intersections of race, class, gender, privilege—you name it—and schooling wasn't new. In the context of the courses I teach, I purposefully cultivate these conversations all the time. It is my hope that my work with students helps them see that contemporary educational debates often reflect longstanding historical and philosophical tensions, and cultivates an understanding that educational problems often are rooted in and symptomatic of social arrangements that extend beyond the classroom and schoolyard. To me, it is my moral imperative to engage my students in the type of dialoguing, advocating, and educating that empowers them to ask critical and difficult questions, that forces them to examine social inequities and imperatives, that challenges them to act in the service of humanity. As well, I hope that students develop the courage, candor, and humility to examine how their own experiences and perspectives impact not just their own development as teachers and school leaders, but the lives of the students in their care as well. Patricia Hinchey (2008) calls this "critical consciousness." I call it essential.

More often than not, these discussions start out in an uncomfortable space. It's not easy to confront privilege, whether you know you have it, think you don't, or witness it at work for others every day. In fact, I can't remember a class in which some permutation of this conversation didn't make everyone squeamish, even just a little bit.

But I'd never been called a "race traitor" before. That was new.

In this particular Foundations of American Education course, I was a White teacher in a graduate classroom full of White students, who by and large taught children who looked and lived very differently from the way they did. The tension had been building for a few weeks. It always does. In various ways and with various materials, we'd discussed how we think about the purposes of education, the role of school as a social institution, the responsibility of the teacher, and the ideal of a "democratic" education. We talked about issues of equity and access, and whether we have different notions of "educatedness" for different kinds of children. We troubled issues of "fair" versus "equal," the allocation of scarce resources, and whether schools reflect or promote a particular social order.

I think it's about there that this particular experience took a decidedly different turn.

Although it would make a more compelling story if I could remember the actual dialogue that made up this exchange, the truth is that it's all a blur. Except for the part where one student, one particularly angry student, said something like, "I don't get it; why are you such a race traitor?" Other students responded with nods and murmurs of agreement. "Yeah, why do you care about those people, and not your own kind?" More nods, and louder murmurs. So I took a deep breath, and we had a conversation.

In retrospect, I'm sure it could have been much worse. The whole group could have been hostile, but that open hostility didn't extend to everyone. Although all of us who have taught in the social foundations have dealt with issues of confronting privilege and discussing difference, this one was different. Every single student in that class, every single one, taught children who were racially and economically different from themselves. And I'm not sure what was more troubling—the very angry student, or the passive acceptance, on the part of everyone else, of what the very angry student said as true.

Shortly after this incident, a couple of colleagues and I signed up for a Ruby Payne seminar. These seminars were based on a self-published book in which she purports to explain the culture of poverty to educators, and they were very popular at the time with school districts. We each had been highly critical of her "framework" (Payne, 2005) but had not experienced it for ourselves. It was there that I witnessed a similar kind of xenophobic sentiment from the facilitators as well as the attendees. It strengthened my resolve to seek to develop in each and every one of my students (the majority of whom are and will continue to be White and female) a sense of critical consciousness. I might not be able to singlehandedly change the demographics of the teaching force, but I can do everything in my power to ensure that the students in my care don't operate on assumptions and perpetuate harmful stereotypes.

Rejected by Referendum by Isabel Nuñez

In his speech accepting the Division B Lifetime Achievement Award at the 2010 American Educational Research Association (AERA) annual meeting, Dr. Thomas Barone asked his listeners to please not boycott the upcoming Narrative, Arts-Based, and "Post" Approaches to Social Research Conference because it was being held at Arizona State University. That state recently had passed Arizona Senate Bill 1070, requiring immigrants to physically possess documentation of their legal status at all times and allowing police to detain anyone they suspected might lack such documentation. Many in the AERA audience wore "Guess if I'm Illegal" stickers in protest, and it was likely that many of them would think twice about traveling to Arizona, where Latino politicians had already called for a convention boycott.

As engaged as I was by the conference theme and as much as I would have liked to be there, I couldn't bring myself to attend. If I am honest with myself, though, my deepest reasons were not about political protest, but instead about fear and hurt. As a dark-skinned Latina with indigenous features, I could easily imagine myself being questioned about my immigration status by Arizona law enforcement. Although I likely would have been in possession of acceptable identification, the experience was still painful in my mind's eye. I felt like my physiology had been determined by a majority of Arizona's voters to be an undesirable presence. Prior to the law's passage, I visited Sedona every year or so for nearly a decade, but I don't know if I will ever return.

I remember the same kind of fear and hurt in a much more vulnerable population in 1994. I was then a 1st-grade teacher in Los Angeles during the campaign for Proposition 187, the successful California ballot initiative denying any social services to undocumented immigrants. The law eventually was found unconstitutional, but the intensity of anti-immigrant sentiment engendered by the campaign was palpable to even the youngest Latino residents of our state. A colleague shared with me how one of her kindergartners raised his hand to ask why they said the Pledge of Allegiance, when "*No nos quieren,*" or "They don't want us."

I am an adult U.S. citizen with a PhD who probably has little reason to be afraid of traveling to a state that I don't need to visit anyway. How have the Latino residents of Arizona experienced this? What about those without legal status? What about Latino children, who did not choose to immigrate, whose family members may lack documentation, and whose only home "does not want them"? My heart aches for their pain and confusion, and for the damage we do to our democracy with policies like these.

SUGGESTED READING LIST

Achinstein, B., Ogawa, R. T., Sexton, D., & Freitas, C. (2010). Reclaiming teachers of color: A pressing problem and potential strategy for "hard-to-staff" schools. *Review of Educational Research, 80*(1), 71–107.

This meta-analysis reviewed 70 demographic studies and determined that there is greater overall turnover rate among minority teachers. However, teachers of color are more likely than White teachers to stay at high-need urban schools. Hopefully, the issues that affect minority teacher retention can be positively influenced with changes to school-level policy.

Dewey, J. (1922). *Democracy and education: An introduction to the philosophy of education*. New York, NY: Macmillan.

This is one of the most widely read volumes of the most influential educational philosopher of the modern era. Here, he explains the role that education plays in any kind of group life, but especially in societies governed under democratic principles of shared power.

Gándara, P., & Hopkins, M. (Eds.). (2010). *Forbidden language: English learners and restrictive language policies*. New York, NY: Teachers College Press.

This book compiles research on the outcomes of laws severely restricting the use of native languages other than English in public schools. The studies in the book focus on the three states—California, Arizona, and Massachusetts—that have passed legislation highly destructive to the education of linguistically and culturally diverse children. Each of these policies was the result of a statewide ballot initiative, perhaps the most efficient way to draw on negative public feeling for purposes of lawmaking.

Hannah-Jones, N. (2014, April 16). Segregation now: Investigating America's racial divide. *Propublica*. Available at www.propublica. org/article/segregation-now-full-text

This work of investigative journalism chronicles the resegregation of the schools of Tuscaloosa, Alabama, following the release of the local district from its desegregation consent decree. By focusing on the experiences of one family, the article explores the impact of our societal retreat from the aims of the *Brown* decision, as well as the complex and nuanced factors that have precipitated it.

Jepsen, C., & Rivkin, S. (2002). *Class size reduction, teacher quality and student achievement in California public elementary schools*. San Francisco, CA: Public Policy Institute of California.

This report examines the effects of California's 1996 Class Size Reduction Act on student achievement. The law limited kindergarten through 3rd-grade classes to 20 students.

Unfortunately, the large influx of inexperienced and uncertified teachers, especially in high-need schools that lost experienced teachers to the sudden openings in wealthier districts, hindered expected student gains, especially for minority and low-income students.

Miron, G., Urschel, J. L., Mathis, W. J., & Tornquist, E. (2010). *Schools without diversity: Education management organizations, charter schools and the demographic stratification of the American school system.* Boulder, CO: Education and the Public Interest Center & Education Policy Research Unit. Available at epicpolicy.org/publication/schools-without-diversity

This research brief examines demographic data on 968 charter schools, revealing that charter schools are more racially segregated than their home districts.

Mosteller, F. (1995). The Tennessee study of class size in the early school grades. *The Future of Children, 5*(2), 113–127.

This article describes the largest scale study to date of the effects of reducing class size on student achievement.

Wells, A. S. (2014). *Seeing past the "color-blind" myth of education policy: Addressing racial and ethnic inequality and supporting culturally diverse schools.* Boulder, CO: National Education Policy Center.

This research brief presents evidence that "colorblind" education policies, such as those promoting school choice and test-score-based accountability, institutionalize in schools the larger patterns of racial segregation that shape our society and the composition of our neighborhoods. Here, Wells argues that we need a race-conscious policy agenda designed to integrate our schools and communities so we can reap the societal benefits of diversity.

Curriculum and Pedagogy

On May 15, 2012, Rob Jenkins posted a blog on the *Chronicle of Higher Education* website titled, "Mamas, don't let your babies grow up to be teachers." Readers, hooked by the clever reference to the country-and-western classic lamenting the life of a cowboy, were told some pretty hard truths about the state of K–12 education—thankfully through humor. The author, a college professor, had spent time on high school campuses and learned that the current state of teachers' working conditions, coupled with the disrespect shown them in the public conversation, meant he'd prefer his children do anything, anything at all, other than elementary or secondary teaching. He likely isn't the only one.

There have been many, and increasingly rapid, changes to teachers' work in recent years, and we are already seeing their in-progress consequences. Many teachers are leaving the profession, and we worry about the career longevity of those who will choose to teach—if constant disrespect, too few resources, and shaky support is what teaching has come to mean—in the future. Too many new teachers already leave the classroom within the first several years. The difficulties that today's educators are facing are legion, from the large class sizes discussed in the previous chapter to the constant media messages about teachers' incompetence. However, some of the most destructive shifts in policy have been in the area of curriculum, which for many is at the heart of teachers' work.

One of the most powerful moments, for us, of the Chicago teachers' strike of 2012 concerns curriculum. While listening to the local National Public Radio affiliate on the way to work, Isabel heard a story reporting on the agreement that ended the strike. When the union delegates came together to ratify the revised contract, the greatest applause, involving teachers standing up and cheering, was for one provision: Teachers have the right to write their own lesson plans. After a fight that involved wages, class sizes, job security—even a possibly uncompensated extra 2 hours of work per day—teachers were the most joyful about winning the right to some degree of creative control over the curricula in their classrooms.

As discussed in Chapter 2, Illinois law prevented teachers from striking over anything but compensation and some aspects of their working conditions. However, in their public statements regarding Mayor Emanuel's insistence on extending the school day without a corresponding pay increase, the Chicago Teachers Union did manage to bring in the issue of curriculum quality. Instead of the "longer day" demanded by the district, the teachers lobbied for a "better day." In many of the city's schools, pressure to achieve adequate yearly progress (AYP) under NCLB had narrowed the curriculum to little more than reading, math, and science, the three areas in which testing was required under the legislation. The "better day" proposed by teachers in Chicago would bring back the rich array of subject areas—including social studies, art, music, physical education—that poor children are too often denied and that all children deserve.

Of course, Chicago isn't the only place in the United States where students are spending the majority of their time preparing for standardized exams. While test-based pressures on school curricula are probably most destructive in the high-need schools that struggle to make AYP, schools everywhere are suffering negative consequences. We hear from friends and colleagues who are parents in more-privileged schools, as well as those of our graduate students who teach in such communities, that teachers of wealthier students also are being constrained in their curricular choices by the need to constantly raise test scores—in this case from very good to even better. The intensifying focus on teaching and learning the kind of bounded, discrete knowledge and skill sets that can be assessed on a multiple-choice exam has meant moving away from one of our most influential philosophies of educational purpose: that schools should serve primarily to impart the necessary cultural understandings of a united people.

SCHOOLING FOR A SHARED CULTURE

The idea of education as the means by which our nation's cultural heritage can be shared with the youngest generations predates even the notion of universal schooling. The earliest educational institutions in the United States were founded during colonial times—with what was then Harvard College, established only 16 years after the Massachusetts colony itself (Willis, Schubert, Bullough, Kridel, & Holton, 1994). This and other early colleges—as well as the primary and secondary schools at which students were prepared for them—were modeled on the schools of the settlers' place of origin, England, where institutions like Oxford and Cambridge trained young men for lives spent in the academy or the clergy.

In 1642, a description of Harvard's curriculum explained that, along with the Bible, students applied themselves to the Latin and Greek languages, classics, "logic, physics, rhetoric, history, ethics, politics, arithmetic, geometry and astronomy" (Willis et al., 1994, p. 8). The students at these schools were exclusively men, and only a select group of male colonial inhabitants at that. However, these individuals represented the population that was entrusted with preserving the settlers' European cultural heritage in the new world.

One hundred years later in our colonial history, none other than Benjamin Franklin, the ultimate practical man, would propose that schools might work to enable a broader range of future endeavors—and do so by offering instruction with real-world applicability and relevance. For example, he recommended instruction in modern, rather than ancient, languages for students planning to go into business (Willis et al., 1994). Still, the commitment on the part of many American educators to a curriculum based on the great ideas and classic texts of Western culture has persisted even until today. Referred to by Schubert as "intellectual traditionalists" and by others (Oliva & Gordon, 2013; Ornstein, 2015) as "perennialists," these individuals believe that a shared foundation in cultural knowledge is necessary for the members of a society to engage with one another productively. They also believe that the schools are where that foundation is to be built.

Some of these scholars are quite influential public intellectuals. For example, during a period known as the "culture wars," Alan Bloom (1987) and E. D. Hirsch (1987) each wrote bestselling books strongly advocating the universal adoption of a traditional liberal arts curriculum. Bloom assumed the stance of critic, bemoaning the "closing of the American mind" as a result of cultural relativism's influence in the schools, while Hirsch took the prescriptive approach, detailing what "every American needs to know" in or-der to be "culturally literate." When one considers the endangered state of multicultural education as described in the previous chap-ter, it would appear that their side "won" the culture wars. How-ever, a look at the larger educational landscape, where the value of a liberal arts education—traditional or otherwise—is being ques-tioned not just for high school but for college graduates as well, shows that perennialism is not the philosophical perspective that is presently driving U.S. education policy.

In fact, while Hirsch's later work in developing and dissemi-nating the Core Knowledge curriculum (Core Knowledge Foun-dation, 1999; Hirsch, 1993) can be thought of a precursor to the Common Core State Standards (CCSS), to be discussed later in the chapter, it is clear that the currently ascendant belief about the purpose of education is not the intellectual traditionalist's. In-stead, it is the descendants of Franklin, with his emphasis on prac-ticality and his faith in science, whose views now hold sway in education policy circles.

TESTING

Nowhere is the dominance of scientific rationality so apparent as in the current national obsession with standardized testing, one of the biggest issues spurring Chicago teachers during the 2012 strike and one of the greatest challenges facing all teachers and students in U.S. classrooms today. Testing is another area in which a his-torical view of instruction is helpful. Large-scale educational test-ing emerged at a particular time in our societal evolution: the late 19th- and early 20th-century scientific and industrial revolutions. At that time, advances in measurement theory and application, along with a growing faith in the potential of empirical science to arrive at objective "truth," opened the door for tests to play a larger role in education (Kliebard, 2004).

Arguably, the shift from an economy based on agriculture and small commerce to one based on the mass manufacture of uniform products made the expanded role of testing appropriate. After all, if students' future work was to consist of standardized, re-petitive tasks, why shouldn't their educational experience involve the same? Such an assertion is undermined when one considers education as more than job preparation, but if schools do exist to get students ready for their work lives, the case for large-scale testing today really falls apart. Manufacturing jobs have all but disappeared from our shores, and the flexible, creative, collaborative knowledge work in which today's graduates will need to be adept, if they are to be successful, cannot be evaluated with a standardized exam.

If this weren't problematic enough, the way tests presently are being used is breaking many of the most fundamental rules of the science in which we proclaim to have so much faith. The first important consideration in the enterprise of testing is purpose. It is imperative that both developers and users of tests are absolutely clear about what is being measured and how the results will be applied in making decisions. The process of test construction is so specialized that an instrument designed for one purpose cannot be effectively utilized for another.

For example, a very important consideration is norm referencing, the system by which a test-taker's performance can be ranked among that of all other test-takers. Norm referencing serves certain measurement purposes well. Some would argue that college entrance exam results, for instance, are appropriately reported this way, as there are limited slots and it is important to know which students are most deserving of them. Norm-referenced scores often are reported as a percentile, where an 87th percentile ranking means that 87% of test-takers received a lower score (a strong result for the individual test-taker), and a 10th percentile ranking means that only 10% of others performed worse (a weak showing for the individual test-taker). Scores also can be reported as an age- or grade-level equivalent, where a result of 5 years 2 months means the test-taker performed the same as the average child of 5 years and 2 months of age, and a 1.9 grade equivalent means that the test-taker's score matched the average attained by 1st-graders in their 9th month of school. (The relative strength of these scores would depend, of course, on the age and grade levels of the test-takers.)

Individual items on exams whose scores are to be norm referenced must be painstakingly written and piloted. This is why many of us will recall seeing on such tests language identifying particular questions that will not affect scores. One reason these questions are given a trial run is to ensure that about half of test-takers answer them correctly and about half get them wrong.

Questions that too many people miss, or that too many get right, do not contribute to the spread of scores that will allow performance to be ranked in this way.

It is not difficult to see why norm referencing is highly inappropriate for tests whose purpose does not involve ranking, such as those to determine AYP for NCLB reporting or those determining promotion to the next grade. For one, these tests should be measuring the performance of students in relation to the standards, not in relation to other students. If norm-referenced scores were used for these purposes, it would be mathematically impossible for all schools to achieve success, and a large proportion of our students would be guaranteed to be held back at each testing threshold. After all, 50% of students will *always* score below the 50th percentile, even if all students achieve unprecedented mastery of the material. Some of us learned this the hard way when professors graded "on the curve" in college. The lesson: Unless you are a *very* well-rounded English major, you should not take chemistry with the pre-med students.

In an attempt to address this mismatch in purpose, some large-scale tests, such as the one used to report AYP by Illinois elementary schools (the ISAT), also offer reporting of performance in relation to the material, a scoring system termed criterion referencing. However, the fact that the test was developed to be norm referenced means that each item was tailored for half correct/half incorrect responses, and countless items that better assessed the standards were rejected. Some scholars posit that the variance of responses in norm-referenced test items is achieved only by requiring knowledge that is not part of the standards, information that students gain through their out-of-school experience and that is not learned in the classroom—no matter how hardworking the teacher and pupils (Kohn, 2004). Readers likely can imagine which students have the requisite kinds of experience.

Another fundamental principle in psychometrics is reliability, which is defined most simply as "the consistency with which a test measures whatever it's measuring" (Popham, 2011, p. 61). A test that produced widely varying measures of the same ability (when that ability was not expected to change) would quickly lose the trust of users. For this reason, test developers work very hard to ensure that their products are reliable. However, it is an undisputed truth in the measurement field that no test is completely reliable. In other words: "Some degree of inconsistency is present in all measurement procedures" (Thorndike, 1997, p. 96).

Psychometricians (scientists of measurement) conceptualize this as the difference between a test-taker's true score (a perfectly accurate reflection of ability, necessarily hypothetical given the limitations of measurement) and the attained score on a test. The difference is called "error of measurement," and it is a component of *every* test score. This is why results are often accompanied by a range representing the standard error of measurement, or an estimate of how much a particular test-taker's score is likely to vary. Public opinion poll results often are reported with similar numbers representing the margin of sampling error, as in "preferred by 36% of U.S. households, plus or minus 4%." This means that the actual percentage of households is likely to be as high as 40% or as low as 32%. It would be psychometrically unsound—not to mention unfair and a misrepresentation—to make a decision that wouldn't be supported by a score anywhere within this range.

Because measurement experts understand the limitations of tests, there is universal agreement in the field on a caveat for their use: *No big decision should ever be made based on a single test score.* This principle is espoused by test developers, governmental bodies, and professional associations alike (National Research Council, 1999). Yet it continues to be countermanded by education policy and practice in the new age of test-based accountability. Tests have "come to define our relationship to questions of truth, knowledge and even reality" (Ronell, 2005, p. 17), and the results are devastating. As teachers internalize the shame of our failure to raise scores, we are more and more fearful of speaking out against policies that we can see are harmful to our students' learning (Taubman, 2009).

COMMON CORE

The next policy issue seems initially to reflect the continued influence of the intellectual traditionalist perspective on educational purpose. It appears to be common sense to assume that a shared cultural foundation is more readily achieved by the time a student graduates from high school if primary and secondary classrooms across the nation are pursuing the same objectives for learning. The Common Core State Standards, published in 2010, have now been adopted by 45 states and the District of Columbia (Kornhaber, Griffith, & Tyler, 2014). Since the U.S. Constitution explicitly leaves education in the hands of the states, the CCSS are ostensibly not a federal initiative. To protect this impression, President Obama was asked specifically not to make Race to the Top grants contingent on state adoption of the standards (McDonnell & Weatherford, 2013). Nevertheless, the CCSS are very nearly a national curriculum policy.

The standards brought together a wide range of disparate supporters, including state governors, think tanks, teachers unions, parent groups, philanthropic organizations, and civil rights groups (McDonnell & Weatherford, 2013). Common Core advocates demonstrated remarkable political skill in managing the varied agendas present among their supporters. Their tactics included presenting different statistical evidence for different groups. For example, a chart showing that states with the largest achievement gaps among student subgroups had the lowest standards was shown to civil rights groups, but not to the business community (McDonnell & Weatherford, 2013). While a broad array of interest groups was successfully united around the CCSS and the mission of raising expectations for students, the research evidence is not in agreement on whether a need for enhanced rigor really exists.

For example, the writers of the English Language Arts Standards explicitly point to a decline in the complexity of student reading materials over the past 50 years. However, an analysis of 117 textbook series published over the past 100 years shows that text complexity has increased or stabilized—there has been no decline at all (Gamson, Lu, & Eckert, 2013). Another language arts feature of the CCSS is "close reading" of texts, or intense analysis bounded by the work itself, which is presented as more valuable than the personal connections a student can make to a reading. However, some researchers argue that close reading works against the deeper understanding fostered when students bring their own experience to bear on what they read (Ferguson, 2013). There is a great deal of research evidence that suggests neither complexity nor any prescribed approach for interacting with a text is a determinative factor in reading achievement. Instead, Krashen (2013) cites national and international qualitative and quantitative studies to show that access to books, as well as time for self-directed engagement with them, is what makes the real difference in reading success.

Regardless of whether the Common Core represents an improvement over present educational practice, it certainly requires significant change (Porter, McMaken, Hwang, & Yong, 2011). The question of improvement is likely unanswerable, depending as it does on a shared definition of quality. Are "harder" standards necessarily better standards? Do high expectations require that students learn a lot of information, or that what is learned be challenging? Porter et al. (2011) compared the CCSS with the standards and assessments of over half the states and found that curriculum will need a great deal of revision in response to the adoption of the Common Core, in regard to both the range of topics covered and the level of cognitive demand. This is primarily because, in the past, state standards varied so widely.

This understandably has been perceived as an equity issue for many, especially in light of the earlier mentioned data about the lowest state standards being accompanied by the widest gaps in achievement. If standards set the minimum target for student learning, it makes sense that educational equity would be served by raising that bar as high as possible. A tremendous amount of philanthropic money has gone into the development, promotion, and implementation of the Common Core, perhaps for this reason. The Gates Foundation alone has donated $200 million to a variety of groups at every stage of the policy process (McDonnell & Weatherford, 2013).

However, some researchers question whether the standards will really help to even the playing field. They suspect that, in stark contrast to the hopes of civil rights groups who were instrumental in supporting them, the CCSS may further harm the students who are already behind. Kornhaber et al. (2014) interviewed "policy entrepreneurs" central to the Common Core initiative and found that most were concerned with equity in education. However, they primarily held the "equal conception" of educational equity, which is concerned only with the provision of equal resources. In contrast to the "equalizing" and "expansive" conceptions, which offer compensatory resources (the latter in out-of-school settings), the equal conception does nothing to decouple achievement from socioeconomic status. Since the standards are now the same, the authors of this study worry that arguments for pure meritocracy will be strengthened, while disadvantaged students will continue to struggle.

Disagreement also exists within the education community about how the Common Core State Standards will affect the work of teachers. Many of our own teacher education students welcome the standards as a respite from the pressure they faced in trying to cover the Illinois State Learning Standards, which they believed included too much content and did not allow for enough depth. This perspective has support in the research as well, with some critics of neoliberal reform in education expressing hope for the possibilities offered by the Common Core. Greater teacher freedom, along with close reading of complex texts (and the fact that some CCSS recommendations come from outside the traditional canon), has been hailed as enhancing the potential for a multicultural approach to teaching (Wells, 2014). Other scholars hold that any standardization or top-down imposition in the area of curriculum development is a threat to teacher professionalism and collaboration among school faculties in creatively meeting the needs of their students (Brooks & Dietz, 2013). Like the question of whether the standards enhance or compromise educational quality, this depends on what the particular state had in place before they were adopted.

Whatever freedoms the standards themselves offer teachers, professional autonomy is undermined by the growing reliance of schools and districts on mass market curricular materials. Corporate educational publishers are already offering a vast array of Common Core–aligned resources for students, parents, schools, and districts. In adopting states, K–12 educators are already worried about whether their textbooks and teachers' guides will help their students master the standards. The CCSS are a boon to education-focused companies, in that they call for pretty much all the public schools in adopting states to completely replace their stores of textbooks and other teaching materials. One of the most profitable of these product lines is the standardized tests that will be used to gauge student learning of the standards—especially since the high stakes attached to the tests ensure robust demand for all the other products. Testing was already a multibillion-dollar industry under NCLB, and the CCSS allow for greatly improved economies of scale in product development (Stedman, 2014).

It is this aspect of the CCSS that has met with the most resistance from some quarters. Standardized test scores, despite their problems and limitations, are again being touted as the only option for assessing student mastery of the new standards—defying the logical assumption that a more intellectually challenging curriculum would require a measurement instrument more nuanced and sophisticated than the multiple-choice test. The issue has even created conflict within organizations that were instrumental in supporting the standards, notably the National Parent Teacher Association (PTA). In a survey conducted by the New York State PTA, two-thirds of parents stated that they were opposed to the Common Core, with two-thirds of these citing the "student testing involved" as the reason for their lack of support. This is unsurprising when one considers the 88% of parents in the same survey who said their children already experience too much testing and test preparation in school (Aloise, Longhurst, & Platin, 2014).

Other voices critical of the standards are conservative supporters of states' rights, who are generally unconvinced that this is not a federal government takeover of schooling. Despite the controversies and challenges, some argue that the Common Core State Standards do support the vision of education held by the intellectual traditionalist, that the experience of schooling will instill each of our students with the foundations of a shared cultural heritage. However, even this premise is questioned. According to Zhao (2012), homogenization of curriculum merely ensures cultural stagnation, as the students who would excel in the yet-undiscovered domains of a more fluid, teacher- and student-driven curriculum instead are marginalized by traditional subject areas.

TEACHER DESKILLING

A 2nd-grade teacher in Rhode Island wasn't allowed to read his carefully prepared resignation letter to the school board, so he explained the destructive effects of a rigidly prescribed curriculum in an Internet video instead, sharing with the world his sadness about leaving the classroom. After 40 years as an educator, a high school social studies teacher in New York left his job to escape "conformity, standardization, testing and a zombie-like adherence to the shallow and generic Common Core" (Strauss, 2013), publishing his letter online. A 4th-grade teacher in Illinois explained in a YouTube video that she was quitting because she no longer had professional autonomy and because "everything I love about teaching is extinct" (Gates, 2013). Another letter of resignation on the Web described the top-down hierarchy and relentless testing that drove the North Carolina writer from her classroom.

These are only a few of the countless testimonials from resigning teachers that have "gone viral" in the education community in just the past couple of years. Watching the education blogs and listserv messages, one encounters them regularly. As many commentators have noted in reposting the statements, these are not the kind of teachers we want to see leaving the classroom—not if student engagement and learning are indeed what we desire. To a person, these educators describe a level of artistry in their craft and commitment to their students that any parent would rejoice at seeing in their own child's teacher. Tragically, each then describes how that creativity, and even that concern, has been quashed by recent changes in education policy. These are individuals for whom teaching is not just a career, but a vocation. For many such teachers, the deskilling of the profession has made it impossible to remain in the classroom.

By far the most common theme in the teacher resignations described above is the relentless pressure teachers feel to raise test scores. Despite the fact that tests include only a small sample of the learning we want for our students, and that their scores can allow us only to make inferences about students' overall achievement, they have become the most important, and in many cases the sole, measure of students' success (and teachers' success, as will be explained in Chapter 6). As a direct result of this, teachers have narrowed the scope of their instruction to those discrete "knowledges" and skills that are likely to show up on a multiple-choice test question. Unfortunately for students and teachers alike, this means less time to develop the more sophisticated abilities that a test can't measure: making connections to other subject areas, real-world application of learning, critical examination of the material from multiple perspectives, creative extension of the concepts, and much more. Instead, substantial classroom time is being spent purely on test preparation, including examination skills wholly unrelated to meaningful learning, such as the mechanics of bubble-filling in the early years and test tricks and tips later on.

The pressure of high-stakes testing is not the only way that teachers' autonomy in their practice is being compromised, although it is strongly related to most of the others. In the discussion of the Common Core above, we observed that the initiative occasioned a wave of CCSS-aligned packaged curricular materials.

However, such resources were already quite common (if not yet Common Core). The state standards that preceded the CCSS were already dictating the content taught, and publishers were already selling products that promised to ensure that all the standards were addressed. Many of the practicing teachers in our courses describe being required to use only the mandated curriculum, which is usually from a commercial vendor. Moreover, our students have been told they must teach these programs "with fidelity"—including the scripted instruction that some of them feature!

This is a contrast to when the authors were in K–12 classrooms. Those were the days before standardization, even before state standards in California. There, I, Isabel, was guided by the California State Frameworks. In a little over 200 pages each, these volumes present the broad goals of instruction for a particular subject area for kindergarten through grade 12. For example, the *Science Framework* (California State Board of Education, 1990) separates content into the physical, earth, and life sciences; frames questions that should guide exploration of the content at all levels; and presents a brief discussion of how each might be addressed in grades K–3, 3–6, 6–9, and 9–12. With this level of flexibility in the curricular guidance for each subject, I was free to construct an educational program that would meet the needs and engage the interests of each unique group of students I encountered each year.

Recent education policy shifts show that teachers are not trusted to design their own curricula, and neither are they trusted to design their own approaches to differentiating instruction. In 2004, the Individuals with Disabilities Education Act was reauthorized, and it included a mandate for Response to Intervention (RtI). RtI was designed to replace the earlier discrepancy model of identifying students in need of special education services, which involved assessing a student's IQ and his or her academic performance, then providing services only when the gap between these grew large enough. There were many problems with this model, not least of which was that many students needed to fall very far behind before being considered eligible for services.

Response to Intervention, by contrast, sets up a structure through which struggling students get help immediately. Teachers are required to assess their entire class on a regular basis, then to group their students according to tiers. Tier 1 should consist of most of the class, who do well with the teacher's regular instruction. Tier 2 students need additional help in the form of mild to moderate small-group "interventions." Tier 3 students need more intensive and targeted instructional interventions. Tier 3 students who continue to struggle may be in need of special education services (Fuchs & Fuchs, 2006). None of this is inherently objectionable. In fact, this is a structured approach to what good teachers do intuitively with students of varied ability.

Unfortunately, RtI actually hinders teachers' ability to do this kind of differentiation well. The benchmarking schedule (every 2 weeks) and the required level of documentation mean that teachers are spending more time testing and recording results and less time gauging their students' progress in meaningful ways. In addition, interventions are required to be "research-based," which is interpreted to mean that they have been validated through the kind of studies that only large-scale publishers can afford. So, instead of designing the additional instructional activities that will meet the unique need of their struggling students, teachers have to select from predetermined lists of commercial products to use with their Tier 2 and Tier 3 groups. As a result, there has been an intensifying focus on easily tested skills—so much so that some researchers are calling for RtI to embrace "other, functional performance criteria" (Daly, Martens, Barnett, Witt, & Olson, 2007, p. 562).

The effort to deskill teachers has been so successful that there is a growing public perception that teachers actually do not possess any specialized expertise. One of the most visible signs of this is in the proliferation of alternative—and particularly accelerated—routes to teacher certification. Since 1984, approximately half a million individuals have begun teaching in U.S. public schools without traditional preparation coursework and field experiences, up to half of all new teachers in some states (Milner, 2013). The best known of these programs, Teach for America (TFA), boasts of recruiting teachers only from the most elite universities. However, TFA teachers do no better than other "fast-tracked" teachers with their students, who significantly underperform the pupils of traditionally credentialed teachers (Laczko-Kerr & Berliner, 2002).

Despite the weak showing of Teach for America recruits in U.S. classrooms, the program has been widely replicated by the international organization Teach for All. Similar programs exist throughout the world, as yet another indicator of the global homogenization of education that Zhao (2012) warns of. When standardized curricula are driven by international high-stakes exams and delivered by teachers who have not studied the history and philosophy of education, or learning science and pedagogy, the role of schooling in preserving and transmitting a national cultural heritage is seriously compromised. When the world's students are preparing for the Programme for International Student Assessment (PISA), and their teachers have no common foundation in the art and science of their vocations, we lose sight of the vision of the intellectual traditionalist.

ENRICHING THE EDUCATIONAL EXPERIENCE

Chicago's teachers resisted a longer school day that promised more drill-and-skill and more test preparation. Both students and teachers deserve to spend their days at school—regardless of how many instructional minutes in each—in deep exploration of our cultures: that of the United States, with all of the diverse ethnicities and origins that it comprises; those of our own unique family backgrounds; and those of the global community we are all a part of. As global citizens, our cultural heritage is multifaceted.

If we are to be enriched by all that schooling for a shared culture has to offer, we likely will need to lessen our focus on standardized tests as the primary means of determining whether students, teachers, and schools are successful. If we can free ourselves from the tyranny of test scores, we will be much better positioned to take advantage of what the Common Core State Standards have to offer in terms of cultural enrichment—and to leave them behind if they don't serve in this way. Instead of standardized tests, we could invest and trust in the wisdom and experience of teachers for both the instruction and evaluation of student learning. After all, teachers gauge their students' understanding in myriad ways every day in the classroom. In this way, we might draw on the great cultural achievements of all of humanity, as well as the professional expertise of educators. By rethinking recent policy shifts in the area of curriculum and pedagogy, we can ensure that our schools help to build a shared cultural heritage.

Creating Curriculum by Isabel Nuñez

I was hired to teach 1st grade on what was called an emergency credential and hadn't been trained as a teacher.

I'd graduated from law school at the University of California, Los Angeles, the previous spring, having learned over my 3 years there that I definitely did not want to practice law. On days that I didn't attend classes, I was substitute teaching and I thought I'd keep subbing until I figured out what to do next. After about a month of this, the principal at one of my regular schools called to say there'd been an influx of English-speaking 1st-graders, and asked me to start a class of my own. The janitor cleaned out a classroom that had been used for storage, and we started the next Monday.

I had no idea what I was supposed to be teaching my kids. The school hadn't planned for the extra class and didn't have materials for us until a month or so later. Every night I agonized over what we would do the next day. The results were not pretty. Let's just say the kids suffered through some pretty dry phonics lessons, lots of letter sounds, and spelling practice. I did read storybooks every day, though. I also kept my eyes and ears open in the lounge and in other teachers' classrooms for good ideas. I ended the year feeling that, while it could have been worse, I did not want to go through last-minute-lesson-plan panic again.

That summer, I gathered a copy of the literature text I'd have for the fall, a list of storybooks, our math workbook, and all the materials I'd collected throughout the year. I lived in a loft space in downtown Los Angeles, and there was plenty of room to spread it all out around me on the floor. I laid a length of butcher paper in the center, drawing rows and columns with a pencil and a yardstick. The columns were the subject areas I wanted to teach: science, math, social studies, storybooks, reading, phonics, punctuation/ grammar, writing, art appreciation, art production, and physical education. The rows were units of time: trimesters and weeks.

I had begun attending all-day workshops on elementary science education one Saturday a month, so this was my favorite subject at the moment and the column I decided to work on first. As I started putting together children's books and science topics (Leo Lionni's *Swimmy* for fish, Lynne Cherry's *The Kapok Tree* for rain forests, etc.), I was struck by an intriguing possibility: Why stop there? I suddenly was reminded of a strange and wonderful thing that had happened to me in the fall semester of my junior year at the University of Southern California. That term I'd taken five courses, in a few different departments, as I hadn't decided on a major quite yet (political science, public administration, and the eventual degree field, English). I worked 37.5 hours a week at a downtown department store, had an intense romantic relationship, and was active in student organizations. Maybe I hadn't had time to think about my classes separately, but when I took my finals that winter I ended up writing essays in every exam that referenced each of my other classes. It was as if the walls suddenly came down from between these disciplines (which admittedly are related, but it was still a powerful realization). Since that time I have never stopped looking for connections, and finding illumination in every area of life in the oddest places.

The possibility I saw on the floor of my loft space was to try to provoke the same realization in my students. I wanted them to know at 6 years old what it had taken me until my 3rd year of college to learn: All knowledge is interrelated. I called this a "comprehensive integrated worldview," and it became my primary curricular objective.

I still used science as my thematic center, deciding to begin with biology and human anatomy in particular. This would fit well with an initial social studies focus on the self, which would move to families and homes right about the time science moved to animals, including pets, parents and their young, and habitats. It wasn't always possible to fit every piece of content together perfectly, but I searched out all the connections I could. Sometimes it worked out beautifully. When we studied the molecular structure of matter, we also looked at pointillist paintings (and made some dot-pictures with thin felt-tipped markers), so the children could see how something "big" can be made of teeny tiny things. If links were harder to find, there still weren't disconnected single-subject activities. If it didn't touch on science, math would relate to social studies, or involve writing. Each year I made or found more instructional materials, refined old lessons, or thought up new ones. The creative intellectual work of curriculum construction was the very best part of a job that I loved in every way.

Including Alex by Isabel Nuñez

Early in my 3rd year of teaching 1st grade in a Mexican American community in southeastern Los Angeles County, I met the person who would have the single greatest influence on my classroom environment. School had already started that day, and we were gathered on the rug for the opening activities when the counselor walked him in and said he'd be joining our class. He introduced himself as Alex, and Alex is what we called him. Later the counselor told me that Alex was his gang nickname and that if we called him by his given name of Christopher (both pseudonyms here), his behavior probably would be better. By then it was too late; he was already Alex in our classroom community.

Maybe the counselor was right, and "Christopher" would have been less exhausting. Regardless of what he was supposed to be doing, Alex was all over the room, crawling under tables and climbing over them, tearing student work and decorations off the walls. It was very difficult to understand him when he spoke. His voice was high-pitched, and his vocabulary and mean length of utterance were more typical of a 3-year-old than a 1st-grader. On that first day, I noticed that each of his tiny teeth was capped in silver, although I don't know what, if any, effect this might have had on his speech.

No matter what kind of reward I promised, I could not get him to do any academic work with me. He would not sit and turn the pages of a book. He would not trace letters or numbers. He would not count plastic bears. The only time I got a glimpse of what he was capable of was when he thought I wasn't paying attention. One Friday afternoon when Alex was spending recess with me after some random act of minor violence (not an unusual circumstance), I asked him to help me with caring for our class pets. We had a rat the class had named Abu, and I asked Alex to feed him while I cleaned out his cage. "He needs 20 of these," I said, handing him the bowl and the can of monkey chow. As I shook out the fresh litter, I watched out of the corner of my eye and counted as Alex put exactly 20 pellets in the bowl.

He was also much more likely to engage in schoolwork if another student was helping him (provided I was not watching, of course). Everyone in the class had the opportunity to teach Alex, even the ones who were far below grade level themselves. Alex's learning became every student's responsibility; they all got to feel like the expert on whatever it was they were tutoring him on, and each one experienced the visceral joy of being part of someone else's learning. Even Alex started looking for the satisfaction of being helpful. One day a student at another table mentioned that she'd lost her brown crayon, and Alex promptly brought over his own.

Later, I heard from the counselor that he'd attended only about a month of kindergarten, up until he'd jumped on the outstretched leg of a seated classmate and broken it. After that he was encouraged to sit out the rest of the year at home, since school attendance wasn't legally mandated until 1st grade. I started to see that Alex might have done that, but also to doubt whether he'd done it maliciously. Walking down the hall one day, I saw Alex push the head of the boy walking in front of him into the wall, and then his look of genuine confusion at the boy's tears.

The other students astonished me with how understanding they were of this behavior, and of the lack of ill intent behind it. While I was working with a small group one day, a girl came up to me with a bloody lip and asked if she could go to the nurse for some ice. As I started to write her the pass, I asked what had happened. No response. After a moment I stopped writing and looked at her. When it was clear she wasn't getting the pass without an explanation, she blurted, "Alex hit me but he didn't mean to hurt me and I don't want him to get in trouble, okay?"

Every month I attended Child Study Team meetings to discuss Alex, and every month I shared the stories of the stealth capabilities and open kindnesses he'd shown since the last meeting. I also answered honestly when asked if he had hurt any students in the class. The year before, the team had already begun the process of getting Alex assigned to a special day school. I didn't want him to go, and I argued that he should stay, but the committee decided that the move was for the best. By April he was no longer in my classroom.

The 1st-grade community that had gotten to know Alex was the strongest and most supportive that I had ever taught—and that I ever would. Even after he left, the ethos remained. Each child's learning was everyone's responsibility. Every person assumed the best of intentions in everyone else's words and actions. We all loved and took care of one another. I tried to re-create this in the years that followed, and I had many other good groups, but I never had the same experience in a classroom again.

This story is what comes to mind when I think about inclusion of students with special needs in the general education classroom. I am not an expert on special education (which may be why this important area of education policy does not have its own section heading in this book), and it may well be that Alex was happier and made better academic progress with the special educators at his new school. Selfishly, though, I can't believe that he could have benefited a classroom community there as much as he did me and my 1st-graders in my 3rd year of teaching.

SUGGESTED READING LIST

Daly, E. J., III, Martens, B. K., Barnett, D. Witt, J. C., & Olson, S. C. (2007). Varying intervention delivery in response to intervention: Confronting and resolving challenges with measurement, instruction, and intensity. *School Psychology Review, 36*(4), 562–581.

In this article, the authors, who support Response to Intervention, express their concern about the narrow range of instructional interventions being utilized. Because the most basic of skills are most easily tested, RtI has led to a neglect of performance criteria that are more meaningful in terms of the real-world transfer of school learning. The authors recommend an approach to intervention that links discrete skills to functional applications.

Kornhaber, M., Griffith, K., & Tyler, A. (2014). It's not education by zip code anymore—but what is it? Conceptions of equity under the Common Core. *Education Policy Analysis Archives, 22*(4), 1–26.

This article distinguishes three conceptions of educational equity: the equal, focused on provision of equal resources; the equalizing, which seeks compensatory resources to foster equal outcomes; and the expansive, which calls for addressing both in-school and out-of-school factors in student achievement. The CCSS have been driven by the equal conception and therefore will maintain the current correlations of student socioeconomic background and academic achievement.

McDonnell, L. M., & Weatherford, M. S. (2013). Organized interests and the Common Core. *Educational Researcher, 42*(9), 488–497.

In this article, two political scientists examine the process by which a wide array of disparate groups came together to develop, promote, and implement the Common Core State Standards. Positing that the CCSS supporters gained in both political and policy learning from earlier failed efforts at establishing national standards, the authors describe the skills demonstrated and strategies deployed in protecting the CCSS from significant opposition through the early years of their development.

Milner, H. R., IV. (2013). *Policy reforms and deprofessionalization of teaching.* Boulder, CO: National Education Policy Center.

This report examines the influence of three recent developments in education policy on the professional status of teachers: the use of student test scores in teacher evaluation, the rise of alternative routes to teacher certification, and the Common Core State Standards. While each of these could be framed as a means to increase teacher professionalism, Milner argues that they work to reduce teacher autonomy and lessen appreciation for teachers' expertise.

Popham, W. J. (2011). *Classroom assessment: What teachers need to know* (6th ed.). Boston, MA: Pearson.

This assessment textbook for practicing teachers not only presents practical information on the design, use, and interpretation of a variety of formal and informal instruments and processes for evaluating student learning, but also provides a foundation in psychometric theory. Authored by one of the foremost experts in the field, the book is written in a way that acknowledges the limitations of measurement and with a welcome sense of humor.

Taubman, P. M. (2009). *Teaching by numbers: Deconstructing the discourse of standards and accountability in education.* New York, NY: Routledge.

This powerful book examines the origins, experiences, and outcomes of the accountability-based reforms that have transformed education in the past few decades—and continue to reshape schooling before our eyes. Taubman approaches the task psychologically, considering how the shift in our societal view of teachers and schools was accomplished, as well as how the shame and fear that are the consequences for teachers have successfully kept us from resisting further attacks on public education.

Willis, G., Schubert, W. H., Bullough, R. V., Jr., Kridel, C., & Holton, J. T. (Eds.). (1994). *The American curriculum: A documentary history.* Westport, CT: Praeger.

This edited volume presents a collection of 36 historical curriculum documents, from a 1642 pamphlet describing the rules and coursework at what was then Harvard College, founded just 6 years prior, to the now-infamous *A Nation at Risk* report of 1983. Including policy documents, government reports, and essays by educational scholars, the book provides a history of curriculum and curriculum thought in the United States, allowing the voices of the times to speak for themselves.

Zhao, Y. (2012). *World class learners: Educating creative and entrepreneurial students.* Thousand Oaks, CA: Corwin.

This book contextualizes the U.S. Common Core State Standards within a worldwide movement toward homogenized school curricula driven by international tests like the PISA and Trends in International Mathematics and Science Study. Zhao argues that the standardization of learning is misguided in a global economy characterized by rapid technological advances.

Funding and Governance

In the summer of 2014, our National Public Radio affiliate, WBEZ, hosted a conversation on Chicago's upcoming mayoral election, held in February 2015. The incumbent Rahm Emanuel's political action group (PAC) raised $1 million in 10 days from just eight individuals. Perhaps, said the commentators, this was an attempt to discourage challengers, especially when this group may have included Emanuel's arch-nemesis, Chicago Teachers Union president Karen Lewis. The previous couple of weeks had seen media reports that Lewis was contemplating a run for mayor, along with musings about the kind of campaign season that would ensue, considering that one of the earliest interactions between the two involved heatedly exchanging the F-word. It got worse from there, as the teachers' contract negotiations became the teachers' strike, and the very well-resourced Emanuel balked at compensating teachers more for the work that they do.

Emanuel and Lewis competing for votes in Chicago would have made for an exciting election, even if they did clean up their language in the interest of improving their appeal as candidates. More significant than even the heightened dramatic tension, though, would be the value of the public conversations that could have occurred if Lewis had entered the race. In Chapter 2, we discussed the coalition building undertaken by the CTU as part of the social organizing model of union work. It is not only teachers, but parents, community groups, other public-sector employees, and the working people of Chicago, who stood to have their concerns voiced in debates between Lewis and the current mayor.

Despite the $7.4 million that Emanuel had already raised (which doesn't include the PAC fund), we like to imagine what could have occurred even beyond an action-packed fall and winter. Money isn't everything, after all. In October, Lewis was diagnosed with brain cancer and withdrew as a potential candidate (Sneed, Fitzpatrick,

& Spielman, 2014). Still, it's worth considering the possibilities for transformation that could have emerged for Chicago as a whole under a Mayor Karen Lewis. For us, the most exciting visions consist of what might have happened in our city's schools. As educational philosopher Maxine Greene (1997), whose death we mourned in 2014, advised us, "Imagine not what is necessarily probable or predictable, but what may be conceived as possible."

What if recent years' practice of giving public money to private corporations through tax increment financing was ended, and schools were able to utilize the property taxes owed to them? What if the district's budget was reprioritized, so that less was spent on the central office bureaucracy and more funds were available for instructional uses? What if this included teacher compensation commensurate with the importance of this work to society? What if Chicago Public Schools once again were governed by a representative school board that was elected by the city's residents? What if a professional educator was hired to be the chief executive officer (and went back to being called the superintendent, while we're dreaming)? What if this new leadership had enough trust in school-level administrators and teachers that district oversight could be substantially reduced, rendering the central office budget cuts unproblematic? What if schools serving poor communities had comparable resources to schools serving wealthy ones, or, dare we suggest, even more? What if each school was governed by an elected local school council whose authority was respected by the district? What if CPS, and each school, saw itself as serving the community as a whole, not just its students, and certainly not just its test scores? What if this revised self-concept led one of the country's largest school systems to resist misguided policy mandates from the state and federal governments? What if Chicago's schools became a model for the defense of public schools throughout the nation?

We know this is a long paragraph of dreaming that seems an incredibly far-away vision at the moment—and may not be possible no matter who is serving as Chicago's mayor. Perhaps this is because the educational philosophy that has been ascendant over the past several years holds very little place for daydreams. We are in the hands of the descendants of Benjamin Franklin, the social behaviorists, whose views on the purpose of schooling seem to be driving policy decisions around school funding and governance in the current era.

SCHOOLING FOR EFFICACY AND EFFICIENCY

It is unusual nowadays to hear anyone talk about education as preparation for political life in a democratic system or intellectual life in a shared cultural space, and it has never been commonplace to define education as an engine of social change. Instead, there is a broad consensus on schools as preparing students for economic life in a capitalist system. Even elementary school vision statements are centered on the aim of economic competition in a global market. For example, a quick Google search of "elementary," "school," "vision," "competition," and "market" led us to the Rockingham County Schools (2014) of North Carolina, whose vision is "Empowering all students to compete globally." This district is far from unique.

Pamela and Isabel attended a talk by Gloria Ladson-Billings in Springfield, Illinois, about 6 years ago, in which she recalled visiting a kindergarten classroom in a school with a similar motto displayed prominently on a mural in the central corridor. Curious as to whether they shared this view, she asked the student group why they come to school. In a singsong voice, they answered, "To get a good job," demonstrating agreement with the practical aims of the school vision statement. However, when she proceeded to ask them what a good job was, she was met with confusion. Perhaps the kindergartners were not yet looking ahead to global competitiveness.

The understanding of education as preparation for some quantifiable measure of future success is referred to by Schubert (1996) as social behaviorism, and by others (Oliva & Gordon, 2013; Ornstein, 2015) as essentialism. Schubert likely would offer a defense of this perspective, pointing out that all of us make use of its principles in some situations. He also would note that, while schools currently are focused on workforce preparation, the economic realm is not the only possible place to achieve success. This is true, and social behaviorist aspirations for schooling also look to technological innovation as a measure. This particular expression of creativity (an aim generally associated with the experientialist philosophy), however, is the one most likely to result in personal and societal monetary gain.

A focus on students' future success in the workforce and marketplace is just one way the current educational landscape reflects the social behaviorist perspective. Today's school policies share with essentialism both the destination and the route to get there. This philosophy is grounded in empiricism, the belief in an observable, measurable, and rational world, and guided by an unshakable faith in science. In this view, the only matters worthy of concern are those that can be quantified. From here we get the notion that people's success can be determined through their earnings, and that students' learning, and teachers' teaching, can be gauged through test scores.

Pedagogically, the philosophy is staunchly behaviorist. While movements toward constructivist and child-centered teaching, as well as curricular trends like whole-language literacy approaches and the project method, have offered alternatives at times, the current shift to direct instruction and standardized curricula shows that social behaviorism is indeed the most influential view of education's purpose at this point in history, shaping policy in every area of schooling, from local to global levels. According to Oliva and Gordon (2013), essentialism has been predominant since the 1957 launch of *Sputnik* by the Soviet Union and the resulting fear of American decline on the world stage.

SCHOOL FUNDING

Interestingly, there is one policy outcome we'd expect from a social behaviorist–dominated education paradigm that seems to be missing. If education is important, as proponents of all four approaches would agree, then that importance should be quantifiable. As with "success," the most straightforward measure would appear to be monetary. Yet, we have not seen a significant increase in education budgets relative to other funding priorities. Current "reformers" talk a lot about the impact individual teachers have on students' future success, but educators are still woefully undercompensated compared with those in other professions requiring similar levels of preparation. If anything, teachers' pay is being reduced through attacks on collective bargaining, restructuring of pensions, and retrenchment in contract negotiations. The battle between Rahm Emanuel and Karen Lewis over compensation for Chicago's teachers is a case in point.

The way schools are funded in the United States has always been a source of confusion for us. On the one hand, the idea of equal educational opportunity is prized in this country and would seem to be a prerequisite for the "American dream," which holds that any person can work his or her way up from any degree of disadvantage to any degree of attainment. And on the other hand, there is the way schools are actually funded. One would imagine that providing every student with a realistic chance would require equalization in the distribution of resources: enough additional funding for less advantaged students that their life chances are truly equal to their better-off peers.

It will come as no surprise that schools serving poor communities do not receive more funding than schools serving wealthy ones. Schools are financed in large part through local property taxes—in richer neighborhoods property is more valuable, resulting in a stronger tax base; in poorer communities, lower property values mean lower school-funding levels—as compared with their more privileged neighbors. Here in our home state, two taxpayers sued specifically to protest the unequal tax burden that results from our system of school financing (some argue that they also were seeking fairer school funding), but the suit's dismissal was upheld by the Illinois State Supreme Court (*Carr v. Koch*, 2012). Tax protestors have had better luck elsewhere, as with the 1978 California ballot initiative called the "taxpayer's revolt." Proposition 13 sharply limited the percentage of value local governments could collect in property taxes, and consequently gutted the once-strong system of public education in that state.

There also has been litigation to address the educational inequities that result from our system of school financing, and the key federal case, *Rodriguez v. San Antonio Independent School District*, came before the U.S. Supreme Court in 1973 (Spring, 2011). That ruling holds that property tax–based systems of school financing are not unconstitutional, despite the differences in district funding levels they may produce. The question of how to pay for our nation's schools was left to the states to answer on an individual basis, and outcomes have been as varied as might be expected. Each state has determined for itself to what extent local property taxes will be supplemented by state monies. The federal government contributes a small amount to education funding as well. The particular combination for each state is referred to as its funding formula.

A national Education Law Center report compared the funding formulas of all 50 states, finding that on average local property taxes account for 43.5%, states supply 48.3%, and the federal government contributes 8.2% of the monies that support our public schools (Baker, Sciarra, & Farrie, 2012). As one measure of fairness, individual states' formulas were compared by the amount of additional funding provided to schools serving larger concentrations of poor students, as opposed to schools serving more-privileged populations. The report's authors found that only 17 states actually did provide more resources to the highest-need students through funding formulas categorized as progressive. The strongest of these were Utah, New Jersey, and Ohio. Sixteen states actually had regressive funding formulas, providing more money to districts with fewer poor students. Illinois is among the worst of these, with only Nevada using a more regressive formula. Fifteen states' systems are flat, with no difference in funding between high- and low-poverty districts (pp. 17–18).

A recent innovation in education policy, charter schooling, is putting further strain on some already tight district budgets. Charter schools are publicly funded institutions that are exempted from many state and local regulations in exchange for meeting the goals laid out in their charters. They originally were conceptualized as laboratories for educational innovation by teachers, and many serve this purpose through programs of instruction tailored specifically for the populations they serve. Their numbers are expanding, with enrollments of "over 2 million students in over 6,000 schools in 41 states plus the District of Columbia in the 2012–13 school year" (Batdorff et al., 2014, p. 5).

Charter schools appear to be draining money from some traditional public schools despite the new schools themselves being significantly underresourced. For every student in attendance, charter schools take some percentage of the funds that would have gone to the student's local school district. Here in Illinois, districts can hand over between 75% and 125% (Calia, Barrett, & Valentine, 2011) of this money. It may seem counterintuitive that districts would lose out, since they no longer have to educate that student. However, those "per-pupil" funds also help defray the district's overhead costs, which often are fixed. Also, movement of students in and out of charter schools can disrupt districts' personnel planning, making their teachers more expensive as class sizes get smaller with student transfers to charter schools. In a national survey, 45% of interviewed school district leaders reported a negative financial impact from charter schools, 47% reported no impact, and 8% reported a positive impact (Calia et al., 2011).

However, even if only about half of districts are suffering finan-
cially because of charter schools, most charter schools themselves
are sorely short of resources. Researchers have found significant gaps in funding for charter schools nationwide (Batdorff et
al., 2014). More troubling was another national finding: Charter
schools spend $400 to $1,400 less on instruction per pupil than
traditional public schools (Nelson, Muir, & Drown, 2003). While
there are some reports that private philanthropy can more than
double per-pupil funding at select charter schools in comparison
to their neighborhood school counterparts (Baker & Ferris, 2011),
this is certainly not the case for all, or most, charter schools. Looking strictly at school funding, neither neighborhood school students nor charter school students seem to be benefitting from this
particular policy initiative.

There are undoubtedly more innovations to come. Unfortunately, we suspect they will not lead to either better funded schools
or greater equality in educational opportunity. School "choice" initiatives have already compromised the quality of public education
for many students. The city of Milwaukee's experience with school
vouchers is one example, and will be discussed in detail in Chapter
6 in the section on privatization. A recent report from the Fordham Institute (Brickman, 2014) extends the idea of school choice
and introduces "course choice," through which students will be
allowed to receive credit for classes presented by a "universe" of
possible alternative educational providers, including, of course,
for-profit entities. The coursework would be paid for with public
money, either directly or indirectly reducing the funds allocated to
traditional districts and schools.

SCHOOL ACCOUNTABILITY

Nel Noddings, one of the most influential living philosophers of
education, spoke to a small audience at DePaul University here in
Chicago in the summer of 2014. The most powerful of her many
important points called into question the value of the term *accountability* for our professional purposes, arguing that it is not part of
the "deep structure" of the language of education. She drew a dis-
tinction between that word, which focuses the gaze upward to the
source of authority, and the word *responsibility*, which instead turns
our attention downward, to the students in front of us, as the ultimate reasons why we do what we do in the classroom.

Here at the Center for Policy Studies and Social Justice, we have marveled at how the term *accountability* has come to refer to whether teachers are doing their jobs, and not to encompass whether teachers have been provided with the resources necessary to do them. We are not the only ones. A recent report to Secretary of Education Arne Duncan commissioned by the U.S. House of Representatives called for a redesigned system of governance in which "accountability for equity and excellence should focus on opportunities and resources, as well as student outcomes" and "actors at every level should be empowered and held responsible according to their role, from students and teachers all the way up to state and federal policymakers" (Equity and Excellence Commission, 2013, p. 37). Now if only we could turn these into talking points on the weekly talk shows.

The construction of the term *accountability* to refer only to the job performance of school-level educators—and only as measured by standardized test scores—has been a feat of powerful, repetitive, and insistent public messaging over careful reasoning. And this accomplishment has enabled similarly illogical changes to education policy. It is a triumph of what Kevin Kumashiro (2008) calls "framing" in education, or the intentional shaping of societal perceptions around particular issues. Along with "standards," "sanctions," and "choice," he lists "accountability" as one of the most productive of the frames that originated on the Right wing of the political spectrum and have been influencing education policy decisions for decades (p. 28). We agree and therefore feel it worthwhile to explore the development of this particular frame.

There has long been a sense that teachers are not really doing what they need to be doing—schools either, for that matter. Many historians (Marshall, Sears, & Schubert, 2000; Rippa, 1997; Spring, 2011) locate the impetus for this shared belief in our educational system's inadequacy in the 1957 launch of the first satellite into space—by our arch-rival the Soviet Union. *Sputnik* became the symbol of our national humiliation in science and technology, and of the failure of our teachers and schools. Then, in 1983, the National Commission on Excellence in Education under the Reagan administration released the *Nation at Risk* report, laying the declining U.S. economic power in the global marketplace at the doorsteps of our school buildings. And the scapegoating of teachers for our national woes has not abated. Just a couple of years ago, the Council on Foreign Relations released a report, coauthored by former U.S. Secretary of State Condoleezza Rice, that posited that the dire condition of our schools was putting our national security at risk (Klein & Rice, 2012). Is it any wonder that the American public has rallied behind the movement to hold teachers accountable, when everything that goes wrong seems somehow to be our fault?

While these messages have been pervasive and powerful, they have not gone unchallenged. In 1995, David Berliner and Bruce Biddle published *The Manufactured Crisis*, in which they debunked many of the doomsayers' claims with intensive statistical analysis. Berliner is still at it, recently publishing, with different coauthors, yet another text that takes aim at the purposely spread misconceptions about U.S. schools (Berliner, Glass, & Associates, 2014). He is not alone in this work. It seems that every dubious report that comes out attacking public education, or advocating some neoliberal alternative, is followed in short order by a review from the National Education Policy Center out of the University of Colorado at Boulder. One of the center's many associated scholars patiently will point out the report's errors and omissions, sometimes prompting a reply from the author—which may then result in a response from the reviewer to the author's reply (Adler, 2014)!

Kumashiro (2008) would suggest that we also look behind the frame to discern what purposes are being served by the shared sense that our schools are failing. What has the public consensus on the need for accountability made possible in the education policy landscape? He points to five policy areas that have been served well by Rightist frames constructed around education issues: "tax cuts and privatization, funding and spending restrictions, alternative teacher certification, censorship, and standards and testing" (p. 7). For the "accountability" frame in particular, however, the most expansive policy accomplishments have been in increasing top-down control of the work of districts, schools, and teachers.

TOP-DOWN CONTROL

The concerns we hear from the practicing teachers in our graduate courses make clear how constrained and controlled they feel in their work. "Why do we have to take a course called Curriculum Construction," they ask, "when we're never going to be able to teach a curriculum we create?" It isn't just the "what" anymore, but also the "how" of teaching that is being directed from above, with scripted programs that teachers are expected to implement "with fidelity." Even the norms of the classroom community can no longer be established by the teacher—much less in collaboration with all its members. A suburban teacher shared her disappointment at not being able to have unstructured discussions in her room because her principal wants to see students' hands being raised before they speak at all times. What was striking about this was that the teacher refused to even consider the possibility of conducting conversations one way during observations and another way when she was alone with her students—despite her belief that freer-flowing discussion was better pedagogically for her students.

This story serves to illustrate the culture of surveillance that has emerged in schools in recent years. A researcher in the Chicago Public Schools reveals disturbing levels of control over everyone on district campuses. In addition to the security guards and metal detectors that we've come to expect in urban schools, Alexander Means (2013) describes bar-coded photo IDs that students must display on their persons at all times. Scanning the cards allows access to detailed student records, including class schedules and disciplinary incidents, as well as a means of tracking student movement throughout the day. Interviewed teachers describe conflicting curricular mandates, each strictly enforced, and a relentless push to raise test scores. No wonder his presence in the schools was met with so much suspicion from everyone from students to administrators. "I would often receive the question: 'Are you from the board?' (meaning CPS headquarters downtown). What this meant was: 'Are you here to spy and report on me?'" (p. 48).

A respected principal of a high-performing CPS school published a scathing letter to the editor of the *Chicago Sun-Times* describing how he and his colleagues had been silenced and intimidated by district-level administrators since Rahm Emanuel became mayor (LaRaviere, 2014). Principals in Chicago have been treated poorly for at least a decade longer than Emanuel has been in office (see the "Trickle Down" vignette that accompanies this chapter). The "top" in top-down does seem to be at a different level when a city's schools are controlled by the mayor. As discussed in Chapter 2, Chicago's long history with mayoral control makes it something of a test case, and the result is school policy that does not serve the best interests of most of Chicago's students (Carl, 2009).

Chicago is not the only city with a nationally touted system of mayoral control of the schools. New York, under the powerful former mayor Michael Bloomberg, also pushed through a wide array of changes to school policy. With a similarly tight rein on his city's schools and waving the banner of education reform, Bloomberg remade governance structures, expanded charter and small schools, revised teacher evaluation and compensation, and closed schools (Keheller, 2014). These are similar to the "reforms" that have been undertaken in other metropolitan districts with mayoral control. While some research has determined that the overall impact of these changes has been positive (Keheller, 2014), many studies question whether this approach to school reform actually is improving urban education.

For example, a Pew study of large-scale school closures in six big cities found that they neither saved the districts significant amounts of money nor had much effect on student academic achievement—but they did result in substantial political fallout (Dowdall, 2011). A study of the impacts of school reform in Chicago, New York City, and Washington, DC, all high-profile cities with mayoral control of their schools, reached several disturbing conclusions. These included that "test scores increased less, and achievement gaps grew more, in 'reform' cities than in other urban districts" (Weiss & Long, 2013, p. 3)—this when assessing the practices against their own stated goals using their preferred form of measurement. If the "reform" movement isn't serving to improve student achievement, then whose interests is it serving?

One way to find out is to "follow the money," a tremendous portion of which is now coming from charitable foundations. A recent study found a marked increase in the amounts of money that philanthropic entities are devoting to efforts to influence the education policy conversation—in addition to much improved strategies for doing so (Reckhow & Snyder, 2014). Here in Chicago, Kenneth Saltman (2010) laid out what has been accomplished through "venture philanthropy" in the city: corporatization of public schools, the remaking of school leadership along the business model, and preparation for urban gentrification through the Renaissance 2010 plan for school closures. Judged according to the benefits to profit-making entities, school "reform" under mayoral control suddenly looks to be progress—and this may be acceptable to a social behaviorist view that prioritizes social efficiency writ large without the ideal of success for all students.

If, however, this is not an appropriate aim for education, as it wouldn't be for many, there are alternatives. Community control, while not a panacea, has allowed for impressive educational innovations where it has been tried. In New York City in the late 1960s, three experimental districts led by elected representatives of their communities took idiosyncratic approaches to improving their schools (Lewis, 2013). While local control was not long-lived in New York, present-day policymakers can take lessons from the community-led districts' successes in fostering the interdependence of neighborhoods and schools, as well as the challenges they faced in addressing conflicts with official bureaucracies and teachers unions. The experimental districts' legacy includes empowered and involved neighborhoods, as well as individual leaders who value collaboration with communities.

Here in Chicago, where the governing board of our public school district has been appointed by the mayor since 1995, researchers and community groups have called for a return to an elected representative school board (Lipman & Gutstein, 2011). Among other concerns, they point to increasingly segregated and unequally resourced schools, lack of academic improvement on reliable measures such as the NAEP, and widening achievement gaps between White students and their Black and Latino peers. Another result of mayoral reforms in Chicago is a growing number of "turnaround" schools. These are schools that, due to low performance, are taken over by private groups and are no longer governed by elected local school councils. Despite the significant amount of additional funding that turnaround schools were provided, their scores have lagged far behind those of democratically led campuses among the city's elementary schools (Designs for Change, 2012). Perhaps this is because the first thing that happens in a turnaround school is that the entire faculty and staff are fired, an action with serious potential consequences, as we'll see in the next chapter.

BEYOND THE ECONOMIC

Let's return to the hopeful speculation of earlier in this chapter. What if a Karen Lewis mayoral campaign had sent us back in time to 1983, when Chicago elected its first Black mayor? Harold Washington's chances were similarly dismissed when he announced his bid, but the city's residents defied the establishment

(Kleppner, 1985). Maybe Lewis could have been the first Black woman mayor, and Chicago could have once again shown what is possible post-Daley. Education is only one of the areas in which such an election might have been transformative, but for us it was the most exciting.

It is devastating to let go of these dreams, and to contemplate Chicago's education community without Karen Lewis. But because of Lewis' commitment to democratic governance and shared movement-building, the loss of her candidacy is not as tragic as it might have been. While she will be deeply missed personally, she empowered her fellow teachers, union leaders, and comrades in the struggle to such a degree that the work will continue no matter what.

School policy might come to reflect concerns other than the economic, whether these focus on the future chances of individual students in the workforce, the potential for profit in the education sector, or U.S. competitiveness in the global marketplace. As important as it is to earn a livelihood, we may discover other motivations for our students. Teachers are in an excellent position to do this. In a society in which, as James Gee (2008) points out, "'work' names an abstract commodity that is bought, sold, and negotiated within social institutions, and which generates profit" (p. 112), the work of most teachers is better described as vocation.

Who's Failing Whom? by Gregory Michie

I could see signs of systemic neglect and abandonment all around me: vacant storefronts, foreclosure notices slapped on front doors of numerous homes, a small, unadorned, and untended play lot. As I marched with hundreds of others through several south side neighborhoods in the spring of 2013, protesting the proposed closing of dozens of Chicago Public Schools, it was clear to me that the citizens of these communities had been failed in many ways—and for many years—by those in power.

This round of school closings, which in the end turned out to be the largest in the nation's history, was pitched as a way to save money for the district by shutting down "underutilized" buildings—schools where enrollment had declined over the years. What wasn't said, at least by the mayor and schools' CEO, was that one of the reasons many schools in poor neighborhoods had lost students was the dramatic increase in the number of charter schools. For a decade, district dollars that could have been used to increase funding for struggling neighborhood schools had been diverted to establish unproven charters, some of which were shameless in their efforts to entice families to pull their children out of neighborhood schools. The week before classes started in August 2013, representatives from a nearby, soon-to-open charter passed out colorful brochures to parents, right across the street from my school.

Besides, the fact that schools were slated for closure due to alleged underutilization was no doubt lost on many observers. In years past, numerous Chicago schools had been closed or "turned around" due to "underperformance"—a euphemism that gained favor with reformers to replace the more loaded "school failure." So the particular reason these schools were threatened with closure may not have registered with the general public as much as the idea that closing them was, by definition, a good thing. The slickest thing about the "failing schools" narrative—used almost exclusively in reference to city schools that serve low-income African American and Latino students—is that, in the minds of many politicians and casual onlookers, it doesn't need to be substantiated. It validates conventional wisdom so completely—*of course* urban schools are bad—that it often goes unchallenged.

Other times, facts are simply twisted to fit the "failing schools" storyline. As the debate over whether to close a record number of schools intensified, the *Chicago Tribune* released a survey of city residents that it claimed gave CPS schools a "barely passing" grade. Six out of 10 respondents, the *Tribune* reported, gave the city's schools a grade of C or D. What the newspaper failed to mention, however, was that their analysis was based on a single question about the city's schools as a whole. When asked what grade they would give the particular CPS school that their oldest child actually attended, 74% of respondents said an A or a B. Not exactly "failing."

What gets lost in the conversation about urban school failure is any sense of history, of how we got here, of who failed whom, and why. "Too many of our children have been trapped in underutilized, underresourced schools," said Mayor Rahm Emanuel in the weeks leading up to the 2013 closings. It was a narrative missing a crucial set of actors, a story told strictly in the passive tense. After all, if kids had been trapped for so long, who'd held them captive?

The most troubling part of all this is that the drumbeat of school failure, accompanied by mass public school closings in U.S. cities, opens the door to mass privatization of our country's K–12 educational system. If that happens, we won't only lose school buildings that have long served as sites of hope and uplift in struggling communities. We'll lose a vital piece of our democracy.

Trickle Down by Isabel Nuñez

When I first arrived in this city to begin doctoral studies in curriculum at the University of Illinois at Chicago, I was taken aback by what I saw in the schools I visited. My own teaching experience in U.S. public schools had been in southeastern Los Angeles County. The district served two municipalities, one lower middle class and one upper middle class, and the school where I taught was in the poorest community of them all. I had learned from college classmates who taught for L.A. Unified that working conditions in large urban districts were more challenging than mine. I used to joke that I taught in Nirvana compared with them. Still, it didn't prepare me for the comparison to working in the Chicago Public Schools.

I was a research assistant to a professor who'd been granted a contract for external evaluation of the Chicago Math and Science Initiative (CMSI). This was a curricular reform effort designed to introduce conceptually driven instruction in these disciplines throughout the district, and it was in its pilot stage. Several schools had volunteered to participate early, in either the math or science program, and they were provided a full-time "instructional coach" to aid in the implementation. My position as part of the external evaluation team was in the elementary schools that were piloting the science program. My job was to gather qualitative data on the process by interviewing coaches and administrators, conducting focus groups with teachers, and observing in classrooms.

These were surely not the most troubled schools in the district, seeing as each had volunteered to participate. I did observe wonderful educational practices and supportive collegial relationships at many of the schools. However, I also experienced a feeling of intense top-down control unlike anything I had felt in the elementary schools in Southern California and the United Kingdom where I'd taught previously, or even what I'd heard about from colleagues who worked for the L.A. Unified School District. Teachers seemed far less autonomous in their instructional decisionmaking, and much more concerned with doing what they were supposed to be doing. It may seem like a small thing, but I was shocked and saddened to see teachers "clocking in," as if they were assembly line workers who couldn't be trusted to put in the time they were contracted for—this despite the fact that Chicago's public schoolteachers work an average of 58 hours a week (Bruno et al., 2012).

Even the administrators seemed on edge. The following is an excerpt from a reflexive memo I wrote after talking to a vice principal at an implementing school:

> The interview saddened me. The pressure that this administrator and this school were under was palpable. I don't think she felt free to share about problems with implementation. She may not have even known about them—there were times in the interview that she deferred to the principal's greater involvement with the program. But she likely wouldn't feel free to say this either. The school was supposed to do CMSI, so she needed to say that they were doing it, and that everything was OK. (Nuñez, Mazboudi, Fendt, Stoelinga, & Wenzel, 2005)

It was only after my duties brought me to a district-level meeting on the initiative that I got a better understanding of what I was seeing.

I observed a session being led by a district-level administrator for the principals of the elementary schools that were piloting CMSI. Now, he may have been having a bad day, but the way that this individual spoke to these professional school leaders—principals, for goodness' sake— was appalling. They were treated like children, and not even bright children. Then it began to make sense to me, the feeling I'd gotten that administrators didn't really trust their teachers. How could they, when they were shown no trust themselves? I still feel that the governance of CPS is particularly authoritarian, but it was 1997 when I last taught in California. L.A. Unified might be just as top-down in its current approach. So, for that matter, might be the suburban district where I was a 1st-grade teacher.

SUGGESTED READING LIST

Baker, B., Sciarra, D., & Farrie, D. (2012). *Is school funding fair? A national report card* (2nd ed.). Newark, NJ: Education Law Center.

This report examines the national school finance landscape, concluding that primary and secondary educational systems are decentralized across the country, with concentrated and increasing numbers of students living in poverty. The authors additionally offer an assessment of each state's school funding formula in regard to its fairness.

Berliner, D. C., & Biddle, B. J. (1995). *The manufactured crisis: Myths, fraud, and the attack on America's public schools*. New York, NY: Perseus Books.

This book presents a spirited defense of American education from the even-then-commonplace charges of its failure. The authors conduct intensive analysis of the very evidence that has been used to support these claims, demonstrating that even the limited picture provided by test score trends shows a student population being well served by the nation's teachers and schools.

Berliner, D. C., Glass, G. V., & Associates. (2014). *50 myths and lies that threaten America's public schools: The real crisis in education*. New York, NY: Teachers College Press.

Twenty years later, David Berliner is back to present a similar set of arguments for another generation, this time with Gene Glass and other contributors. In this book, they confront 50 misconceptions about the state of public education in the United States, explaining why each is both untrue and potentially destructive to the good work that is being done by teachers and schools.

Klein, J. I., & Rice, C. (2012). *U.S. education reform and national security*. New York, NY: Council on Foreign Relations Press.

This relatively recent addition to the body of literature on how teachers and schools are ruining our country was coauthored by a former chancellor of the New York City schools and a former U.S. secretary of state. In the report, they describe how the vast swathes of our population who emerge from our schools undereducated are putting not only our economy but our very national security into peril.

Kumashiro, K. K. (2008). *The seduction of common sense: How the Right has framed the debate on America's schools*. New York, NY: Teachers College Press.

In this book, Kevin Kumashiro examines the power of frames to shape public perceptions of educational issues and thereby enable shifts in policy for schools. As the title implies, most of the text is devoted to analysis of Rightist frames, their origins and development, as well as what they have accomplished in terms of education policy. The final chapter offers hope in the form of a vision for progressive framings of educational issues that can be used to defend our public schools.

Means, A. J. (2013). *Schooling in the age of austerity: Urban education and the struggle for democratic life*. New York, NY: Palgrave Macmillan.

This book is based on a qualitative study conducted in a Chicago public high school, but the findings it describes can be extrapolated to campuses around the country serving poor youth of color. In it, Alexander Means reveals a level of surveillance and control that would seem antithetical to life in a free society.

National Commission on Excellence in Education. (1983). *A nation at risk*. Washington, DC: Government Printing Office.

When it comes to the scapegoating of our teachers and schools for all of America's ills, this report may not have started the trend, but it certainly raised the stakes. In it, the commission introduces the now-familiar claim that the inadequacies of our educational system are to blame for the poor performance of the United States in the international economy.

Reckhow, S., & Snyder, J. W. (2014). The expanding role of philanthropy in education politics. *Educational Researcher, 43*(4), 186–195.

This May 2014 article in the flagship publication of the American Educational Research Association explains how foundations have both increased their monetary commitment and strengthened their strategies with regard to influencing school politics and policymaking. More giving, convergent gifts, and monies targeted to nontraditional players in education have allowed philanthropic entities to expand their impact on our nation's schools and how they are run.

Spring, J. (2011). *The politics of American education.* New York, NY: Routledge.

In this book, Joel Spring explores the perspectives and relative influence of the various actors who play a role in educational politics. From politicians and the business community, to parents and teachers, to the media and the public, Spring examines how each of these groups, individually and in combination, has worked to shape education policy, historically and in the present, with regard to a range of school issues.

The Vocation of Teaching

On September 24, 2009, 16-year-old Derrion Albert was beaten to death by fellow students from Fenger High School in Chicago—the brutal murder captured on video and broadcast to a horrified nation. The visual images—and the fact that Albert was an honor student uninvolved in the rivalry that led to the fight and to his death—made this African American young man stand out for some people. But Derrion Albert is one of hundreds of youth who perish unnecessarily each year in the city's disinvested neighborhoods— each a tragedy, each an unspeakable loss, each an exclamation point on failed policies. His demise was a sharp reminder of the violence and loss that have long plagued poor communities in our urban centers.

For teachers in Chicago, however, it wasn't the same old story and it didn't have the same old culprits: the gang members who are the villains on news broadcasts night after night. Chicago teachers knew that culpability for Albert's death lay elsewhere, and that while he suffered the ultimate harm, he was not the first person to be hurt when the circumstances that led to the murder were set in place. In June and July 2009, Fenger lost all but nine of its more than 100 teachers in a policy called school "turnaround" (Schmidt, 2009). Veteran educators who had built relationships with the students and with the community over years of service were dismissed, and a new team of teachers was brought in. At the same time, a nearby high school was remade as a military academy, which sent a large group of former students across neighborhood boundaries to attend school with rival gang members at Fenger.

The disastrous outcome of the collision of these two policy decisions was clearly foreseen by the community and the teachers, who warned CPS in public hearings before the February 2009 turnaround vote. Tragically, the district did not heed the warnings, nor did it learn from what transpired. The purging of school faculties, already well under way at the time of Fenger's turnaround, has continued unabated and even intensified. The massive school closures in Chicago have meant that even more veteran teachers in impoverished communities are no longer in the classroom.

One of the Chicago Teachers Union's key demands in the run-up to the 2012 strike was job security. And this is not just a concern for our local teachers: Chicago is far from the only city where policy reform–driven layoffs have disproportionately affected the educators who have chosen to work with the highest-need students. It is also not alone in seeing veteran educators losing their jobs while younger teachers are brought in, often through alternative certification or Teach for America–type programs.

Thinking back to the previous chapter's philosophical lens, part of the reason for this is almost certainly financial. Younger, less experienced teachers are much less expensive than their veteran counterparts. As a society, we have chosen to allocate resources in particular ways, such as in 2011 putting over half (52%) of federal discretionary spending into defense, with education left to compete with transportation, veterans' benefits, and several other areas for the remaining 48% (Congressional Budget Office, 2011). These choices have consequences, and one of these has been the devastating impact on school funding as state and local government revenues suffer the continuing effects of the economic downturn. A portion of our education budgets is bound to disappear. However, when some of corporate reform advocates' favorite research is touting the extra millions in lifetime earnings for the classes of a strong teacher (Chetty, Friedman, & Rockoff, 2011), replacing experienced teachers with newcomers is not the best financial decision. There is something else going on, and to discern the other reasons we need to examine the policy landscape through a fourth philosophical lens on the purpose of schooling.

SCHOOLING FOR SOCIAL CHANGE

We don't hear them much, but throughout our history there have been voices in education policy arguing that schools should be the catalysts for the betterment of societal structures (Counts, 1932a). In recent years, the education community has been inspired by legendary figures like Paolo Freire (1985) and challenged by critical scholars like Michael Apple (1996). However, such voices do not represent a large portion of public opinion in the United States or hold much sway in policy debates. As a nation, we don't often draw on what Schubert (1996) calls "critical reconstructionism" and others simply term "reconstructionism" (Oliva & Gordon, 2013; Ornstein, 2015): the understanding of education as serving social change. This should come as no surprise, when both historical (Harold Rugg) and more contemporary (Howard Zinn) educators' attempts to share this perspective with students through textbooks have led to accusations of being anti-American. Nevertheless, asking difficult questions is considered by some to be a demonstration of the best of our national character.

When an inquiring, even skeptical, mindset is thought to be an asset to society, teachers become the designated nurturers and guardians of this national resource. Because the social criticism inspired by this approach to teaching almost certainly would raise the ire of powerful people, protections for teachers *in regard to this particular role* were built into education policy. Namely, job security in the form of the tenure system was institutionalized for educators at the elementary, secondary, and postsecondary levels (Spring, 2013) and negotiated through union contracts. Tenure is earned by educators after a set number of years of service, and, once in place, a strict set of procedures is mandated before teachers can lose their jobs. While there have been abuses of the system, tenure's original purpose and primary function have been to preserve the free speech of those who are best placed to inspire the critical questioning of the nation's residents.

Tenure's original purpose is not common knowledge. Even in talking about it with our students, who are all practicing teachers, we hear more disparagement than defense of the tenure system. Every class discussion on the topic involves at least one story of the terrible teacher who was kept in the job because of tenure. Many teachers are unaware not just of the purpose of the tenure system, but of the critical reconstructionist perspective on the purpose of schooling. To a large degree a consequence of the policy changes discussed in previous chapters, there is little curricular space in which students can question our societal institutions. A teacher who is not allowed to think critically through developing her own unique curriculum and pedagogy cannot possibly model critical questioning for her students. The tenure system is under grave threat at present. However, much more than teachers' job security is in danger of being lost—it is the inquiry stance of future generations.

VALUE-ADDED MEASURES IN TEACHER EVALUATION

Any consideration of teachers' job security requires a careful look at
one of the most popular—and hands-down the most frightening—of
the "innovations" in education policy to emerge over the past several years. Often called "value-added," it uses student test scores in
teacher evaluation in an attempt to quantify the effects of a teacher's
work on the educational outcomes of his or her students. The effect
of the "reform" is rapid and random teacher turnover: rapid because
this is a ranking system, where some teachers are always going to
come out at the bottom, and random because the statistical models
are so flawed. There can be no meaningful job protections for teachers if this system is fully implemented.

We probably all could agree that teachers should have a beneficial impact on their students. Otherwise, why have teachers at
all? But, after this, literally everything will need some deeper discussion. Value-added assumes that the particular benefit we most
want teachers to impart is academic advancement (and that teacher impact can be made a discrete variable in a student's learning
and life), but this is not the only possible answer to the question.

As a parent, if I, Isabel, had to choose between the teacher
who would help my shy, hesitant daughter reach the appropriate
learning targets and the one who would instill in her a sense of
confidence, a love of learning, and an expressive voice, I would
choose the latter without hesitation. Sadly, with the effect that recent reforms have had on curriculum and pedagogy, this is often
an either-or proposition. Even when the drill-and-skill approach
to instruction isn't directly destructive of engagement with learning, the pressures of test preparation—intensified when a teacher's evaluation and job depend on it—will make it harder for my
daughter's teachers to really see her and figure out what she needs.
And if, heaven forbid, she ever struggles with more acute nonacademic issues (hunger, homelessness, illness, grief, bullying, trau-
ma, suicidal thoughts), I want more than *anything* for her teacher
to be a caring influence in her life—academic learning be damned.
I want my daughter's teachers to have a beneficial impact on her,
but academic growth is not the be-all and end-all, or even the most
important aspect, of that impact.

Although we would argue that the most important contributions
a teacher makes to a child's life are not necessarily academic, we
know that many believe otherwise. Let's assume that knowledge,

skills, and abilities in the subject areas are the most important learning that students can take away from their experiences in a classroom. This might lead us to embrace value-added—but only if we agree that academic learning is limited to those disciplines that are tested. Right now, in too many districts teachers are being evaluated based on test scores in reading and math only. While this might seem logical for teachers whose instruction is in these two disciplines alone, it is clearly inappropriate for teachers—like those in most elementary school classrooms—who should be teaching many more subjects. When one's job depends on student growth in particular areas alone, concentrating one's efforts on those areas is an understandable response. For those lucky students whose school communities successfully have resisted the NCLB-driven pressures to narrow their curricula to reading and math alone, value-added presents one more threat to the breadth of their learning. Based on what we hear from our students, veteran teachers are less likely to succumb to the temptation to narrow, but this may change if tenure disappears.

Of course, not all teachers work with students in the years that they are tested, and some provide no instruction in reading or math at any point in their work with students. They cannot be fairly evaluated in a system based on value-added. The way that this question has been answered in some states and districts would provide some much-needed comic relief here if people's livelihoods and children's futures weren't at stake. In Tennessee, teachers of nontested subjects and grades take their individual value-added score from whole-school measures (Tennessee Department of Education, n.d.). So, the abysmal music teacher in an academically strong school or the stellar P.E. teacher in a weaker school soars or suffers with the school as a whole: not a fair deal, and directly counter to the notion of individual accountability on which the system supposedly is based. Florida's attempt to base a teacher's unsatisfactory rating on the whole-school performance of a different school that hers feeds into—before any students she actually taught set foot there—led to an administrative order putting the whole system on hold (Florida State Board of Education, 2012). It seems that the noncognitive learning goals we have for our students (e.g., fairness) have been neglected for a while now: The board actually needed a lawsuit to see that the above-mentioned example was unjust.

Advocates of value-added would respond that we can, and soon will, test in more grades and subjects. The assessments to accompany the new Common Core State Standards are already being developed. This is less-than-joyful news, considering the limitations of testing, but it still doesn't address the problem. While these might provide scores for science and social studies (which, therefore, could bring these back into every school's curriculum—a very good thing), they don't give us an appropriate way to determine the value-added for a nonacademic subject like art or dance. We know that statutory, budgetary, and curricular pressures have meant that fewer and fewer students have the opportunity to learn from an art or dance teacher (a tragedy that corporate reformers are unlikely to allow to happen in their kids' schools), but our methods of teacher evaluation still need to fairly assess these contributions. Paper-and-pencil tests are simply inappropriate for the job. If we were to make the mistake of trying to "test" in these subjects, we would end up with a skewed sample of the learning that we hope to see there, which in turn would distort instruction. Instead of creativity, aesthetics, and expression, teachers would focus on discrete knowledge and easily demonstrable skill—to do otherwise would put their jobs at risk.

It isn't difficult to imagine the dangers that high-stakes standardized testing would present to student learning in art and dance, but what we often forget is that the same risks are inherent to testing in any subject area. Construction of any standardized assessment instrument involves taking a sample of all the learning one hopes to see in that discipline. And, just as in the arts, there is more we hope to see than can be captured in a multiple-choice question. For students who are not reading at high levels, whether because of age, ability, or English language fluency, there is no way to gauge the complexity of their thinking with a paper-and-pencil assessment. If we really want to know where they are, we need to use authentic assessments and flesh-and-blood teachers. But even with solid readers, those who can show higher-order thinking through the selection of answer A, B, C, or D (and even if most tests were well designed), there are other, less testable goals we have for learning—even in the core academic subjects. We want our students to appreciate beauty not just in dance but in mathematics as well, and we want them to be creative not only with their art, but with their writing.

Our first priority for every subject, above all other goals, should be enjoyment in learning. Reading engagement, possessed by students with positive affect toward the many kinds of books they read in their free time, is a better correlate to reading scores on the PISA than age or socioeconomic class (Brozo, Shiel, & Topping, 2007). In other words, younger and poorer students who love reading score higher than older and richer students who don't. If we really want to raise achievement, we need to figure out with teachers the many ways to instill student engagement with their subjects. Unfortunately, this is not something you can test for.

All of this is by way of prologue. What is most disturbing about value-added doesn't come into focus until you start looking carefully at the way such measures are formulated. Even if we agree that the limited range of knowledge and skills that can be reflected on a standardized test is all we want for our students, we are simply not at a place in mathematics that allows us to do this fairly. Before the Obama administration announced the rules for the Race to the Top fund in 2009, the U.S. Department of Education received a letter and commentary from the Board on Testing and Assessment of the National Research Council (2009). The board warned that there was not enough research to support the use of value-added measures in teacher evaluation, and strongly cautioned against implementing this aspect of the regulations. President Obama chose not to heed the warning, and since then major professional associations of mathematicians, psychometricians, statisticians, and economists—the people who understand the math—have released similar public documents describing the unreliability of the formulas being used to calculate value-added. We should all listen and pay attention to these warnings.

Even the Educational Testing Service (ETS), a nominally nonprofit organization that nevertheless stands to expand its already substantial influence with every additional use for standardized tests, has called value-added in teacher evaluation an improper use of testing (Braun, 2005). In a policy report, the ETS explains that proponents of value-added are making a common error in the interpretation of statistical information: confusing correlation with causality. Even when teacher "effects" are found, they do not translate to teacher effectiveness. As noted in the ETS report, the biggest statistical impediment to determining teacher effectiveness through value-added is that students are not randomly assigned to teachers, a necessary component for an experimental study.

One study where students were assigned randomly did find significant teacher effects, but even here these effects did not persist in future years' test scores (Kane & Staiger, 2008). This makes it unlikely that a single teacher can add extra millions to students' lifetime earnings, as another study claims (Chetty et al., 2011). Nonrandom assignment irreparably skews value-added. One researcher used value-added formulas to find 5th-grade teachers' effects on 4th-grade students' learning (Rothstein, 2009). Since the 5th-grade teachers hadn't taught the 4th-graders, the effects could not possibly equate to teachers' effectiveness. Instead the effects predict the ways that particular students will be placed into particular teachers' classes. We are not yet hearing arguments that students should be assigned randomly to teachers for the sake of more reliable value-added scores. This would be an educational travesty, since students would no longer be assigned to the teachers best suited to working with them. It would, though, prove once and for all that the goal is *not* better outcomes for students. As it stands, the statistical hurdle of nonrandom assignment is insurmountable, and test scores should not be used in teacher evaluation.

Nonrandom assignment is not the only problem with value-added measures. The Economic Policy Institute (2010) released a briefing paper examining the various ways that socioeconomic status (SES) can affect value-added scores. Acknowledging that value-added formulas measure progress, and so might seem fair to a teacher whose students start out further behind, the authors point out that SES affects not just where students are at the beginning of the school year, but also the rate of their learning. Student mobility, a much bigger challenge in poorer communities, further complicates the process of fairly determining a teacher's value-added—and may cause teachers to neglect highly mobile students, arguably the ones who need the most help. Finally, the issue of summer loss makes the teachers of low-SES children especially vulnerable. High-SES students often demonstrate summer gain from the travel, cultural events, and enrichment experiences provided by their families. Unless tests are given multiple times a year, summer gain/loss is calculated into a year's growth and attributed to teachers, making it less likely that teachers will choose to work in high-need schools and making them particularly insecure in their jobs if they do.

With all of this, it should come as no surprise that the Rand Corporation's overview of value-added models concluded that none of them have a small enough degree of error to make their use in teacher evaluation fair (McCaffrey, Lockwood, Koretz, & Hamilton, 2003). Different statistical formulas use different approaches in an attempt to account for nonteacher influences like the ones described in the paragraph above. The report described a variety of models and located the sources of potential error in each of them. The best districts can do is try to avoid the worst of these errors, but no model was considered acceptable. Yet, despite all of the warnings, the use of test scores in teacher evaluation is growing exponentially.

Advocates admit the statistical limitations—a 26% error rate with 3 years of data, which goes down only to a 12% error rate with 10 years of data, according to the report from the Economic Policy Institute (2010)—but these advocates say that value-added is just one of multiple measures being used to evaluate teachers. This is cold comfort when that measure can be weighted at half or more of a teacher's overall rating. Even more worrisome, however, is the emphasis being placed on the correlation of these multiple measures as evidence of their trustworthiness. Because traditional methods of evaluation (like principal observation) are being tainted as subjective, value-added, with its concrete quantifiability—regardless of how unreliable the derivation—is the measure with which all the others are compared. So even if it is one of many measures, it is the one that counts.

John Ewing (2011), writing for the American Mathematical Society, described value-added as just one more example of "mathematical intimidation." Comparing this deployment of questionable statistics with the use of mathematics for purposes of war, and even with the role of complex math in the financial products that started the recent economic meltdown, Ewing calls upon his colleagues to resist such misappropriation of the tools of their discipline. The research cited here shows that at least some of his fellows are doing just that, but the spread of value-added does not yet seem to be slowing. If it does not abate, we likely will see nothing less than the destruction of the U.S. teaching force through the random and regular turnover that test-score-based evaluations will bring. If there is one policy that teachers need to speak out against with a single voice, it is this one.

UNION BUSTING

The Chicago Teachers Union's fourth demand in the run-up to the 2012 teachers' strike, job security, was largely about fighting the new teacher evaluation plan proposed by the Chicago Public Schools the preceding spring—one that made student test scores central in determining teachers' and principals' ratings. During the strike, the CTU succeeded in negotiating the weight given a teacher's value-added score down to the minimum required by Illinois' Performance Evaluation Review Act. Even though state law made it impossible for the union to completely protect teachers, the union weakened the strength of value-added in evaluations of Chicago teachers. To really advance the project of dismantling the profession, teachers unions will need to be eliminated—or at least disempowered.

This is just where we find ourselves, in the midst of all-out attack on unions. Notice that the assault is not limited to unions representing teachers—unions of all kinds are under fire. My partner's parents regularly watch FOX News. Not that I, Isabel, am any better, getting the bulk of my current events information from National Public Radio. It has been interesting to hear how my in-laws characterize unions. According to them, an acquaintance who has been working his way into the plumbing trade has been ruthlessly blocked by the union from taking lucrative jobs—despite his own patience in earning the union status that one day will reserve those jobs for him *and* ensure he is well compensated. Whether it's pilots and flight attendants breaking the backs of the airlines (and raising our baggage fees), or pensions and health care bankrupting the states, the blame for any sector's economic woes is likely to be laid at the feet of the unions.

Half of the states in the nation are now "right-to-work" states that restrict union activities—more honestly described in President Obama's words as states with the right to work for less money. Despite his critique of these laws, the value-added mandate for Race to the Top eligibility has shown the president to be no friend to teachers unions. Not all of the laws prevent teachers from organizing—the restrictions vary in type and intensity by state. There are only five states, all in the South, that do not permit teachers to bargain collectively (National Council on Teacher Quality, n.d.). NAEP scores, by the way, are significantly poorer for students in states like these without binding teacher contracts (Strauss, 2010b). Defenders of right-to-work legislation, including Right-wing think tanks like the Fordham Institute, express outrage that union dues and agency fees go toward political contributions and lobbying (Zeehandelaar, 2012), and most right-to-work laws prohibit the use of mandatory fees for these purposes. However, the fact that the Chicago Teachers Union was unable to bargain value-added down from the statutory requirement of a 30% weighting shows that a union presence in the statehouse can be critical.

The two national umbrella unions, the American Federation of Teachers (AFT) and the National Education Association (NEA), are in a difficult position right now. Not only has their political influence been curtailed with the slowed flow of money from right-to-work states, but contributions wouldn't go very far anyway—not in our two-party system. Traditionally the unions have backed Democratic candidates, but now the Obama administration arguably has done more damage to the public school system than was accomplished by George W. Bush's signature NCLB legislation. Until there is a sea change in one of the parties—or a new one emerges—teachers would appear to have few allies in politics.

Teachers, and their unions, have always faced a tough negotiation: Is teaching a profession or is it labor? While some aspects of being a teacher, like the educational requirements, point to their status as professionals, other parts, like the modest salaries, would put them in the labor category. The two major unions seem to profess different leanings in regard to this question. The NEA seems to view teachers more as professionals. The first sentence on the "About" page of its website describes it as "the nation's largest professional employee association" (NEA, n.d.). The AFT appears to see teachers more as part of the U.S. labor force. The first sentence on its website's "About" page says that it is "an affiliate of the AFL-CIO" (the American Federation of Labor and Congress of Industrial Organizations) (AFT, n.d.). As teachers lose the control they once had over their work—curriculum, assessments, pedagogical practices—the more teaching moves away from the professions and the closer it moves to labor. As workers, with less autonomy and lower compensation than most other professions, teachers need the collective voice that a strong, labor-oriented union can provide.

Here, the Chicago Teachers Union can be a model. The CTU has held the proud designation of Local 1 of the American Federation of Teachers since it was chartered in 1937, and its present leadership is faithful to that history. The union's precursor organization began as a group of female teachers who fought for pay equal to their male counterparts' under the leadership of the legendary Margaret Haley (Rousmaniere, 2005). President Karen Lewis and her team showed the same passion for justice during the strike and inspired the 32,000-strong membership—and the city itself—to stand with them. The strike wasn't supposed to happen. Jonah Edelman thought he'd broken the union with the 75%-of-membership authorization requirement. But Karen Lewis knew her teachers, and perhaps even knew her city.

If only that was the end of the story. The closure of 49 Chicago Public Schools at the end of the 2012–2013 school year, along with the larger phenomenon of school closings and massive teacher/staff layoffs in urban areas around the country, is dealing yet another blow to teachers unions. Forty-two percent of closed public schools in the United States have been reopened as charter schools (Dowdall & Warner, 2013), and charter schools are not required to hire union teachers or pay union salaries. While some charters do honor union-negotiated contracts, and unions have made some headway in organizing teachers even at highly resistant charter schools, expansion of charter schools is almost sure to weaken teachers unions.

This may not be the worst that teachers unions have to face. We used to find ridiculous-sounding ideas from conservative think tanks funny. Now that we've learned they're likely to turn up as serious policy proposals, we're much less apt to laugh. When we read a report on teachers in the electronic age that envisioned "harnessing the power of technology" to allow all students to experience the most effective teaching, like that in the Kahn Academy online videos (Hassell & Hassell, 2011), we passed it around to friends and colleagues with a facetious message about entering the sci-fi world where we'd have one 1st-grade teacher for the entire country. The report described how "less effective" teachers could move into new roles as lab monitors. Unions, in this new age, would look more like entertainment industry unions, where "stars" command market rates, and "extras" earn a guaranteed minimum wage and benefits. We were aghast when first reading this, but really felt the fear a short while later, when we found out that the CPS personnel office is now called the "Talent Office."

This may read like a dystopian fantasy—indeed, we hope it does. But we need our teachers unions, and all of organized labor, to keep this and other visions of schooling from coming to pass. Even if we don't agree on the critical reconstructionist idea of the purpose of education—to inspire justice-oriented change in society—all the other goals for schooling will be at risk if the ends of the current reform movement are not averted. Whether we believe that schools should nurture individual growth, impart a common culture, or actually prepare *all* children for success, we need to preserve and protect public education.

PRIVATIZATION OF SCHOOLING

Taken as a whole, the education policy reforms that have been discussed throughout this book point in one direction—the end of public education. Among the reformers who are honest about their hopes for the privatization of education, the most convincing are those who truly believe that things will get better with the entrepreneurial freedom a market-based system will allow. This perspective is powerfully presented in the 2010 documentary *Waiting for "Superman."* When we hear these arguments, we are reminded that not every community is sad to see its school close. There are some schools that have been ill-serving poor children for years, even generations.

Several years ago the educator and scholar Angela Valenzuela spoke here in Chicago, telling a story about testifying before the Texas legislature on a voucher bill. She was there to speak against the bill, and as she moved to join her mostly White colleagues on one side of the aisle, she saw that nearly all the speakers on the other side were Latino/a—she was not on the same side of this issue as the people who looked like her. She described going over to talk to them about it, and hearing that those families had been promised better schools for years, for generations, and that they did not have any more time to wait for the promises to be kept. Anything had to be better than what their schools were like now. We've heard many anxious progressives wondering how we can bring more people of color into the fight to save public schools. We need to understand why it will be such a challenge.

We empathize with those who are hopeful that privatization truly will lead to better schools, because we know that the public schools in poor and urban areas have failed on many, many levels. Of course, we would point to policy structures—especially school funding through local property taxes—as the reason for these failures, rather than an inherent problem with the public nature of the system. Still, the need for some kind of radical and dramatic change is undeniable.

More often, though, the voices exhorting privatization do not focus on improved educational outcomes for the most disadvantaged. Many of them aren't motivated by a vision of better schools for anyone—the prize here is profit. Pearson, the biggest education company in the world, had sales of $9.5 billion in 2013. Rupert Murdoch, the media mogul, has spoken of K–12 education in the United States as a "$500 billion sector . . . that is waiting desperately to be transformed" (Klopfer & Haas, 2012, p. 50). For many, especially the biggest players in the education "business," it's about the money.

To us, this is actually putting a good spin on it. We do, after all, live under a capitalist economic system. In such a system, continuous growth is the only acceptable condition, and markets need to keep expanding. On his election, President Barack Obama was clear that health care reform would be his signature achievement. When he chose Arne Duncan, whose accomplishments as CEO of the Chicago Public Schools included the pro-privatization Renaissance 2010 plan (Saltman, 2010), as his secretary of education, we wondered whether medicine was being exchanged for education. Were the health-related profits to be lost to a single-payer system being replaced by the money to be made in schooling? This seemed reasonable. If people were forced to choose, most would prefer to be alive than well educated. But in the end, we did not get a single-payer system, and we are still seeing education being taken over by corporate interests.

More disturbingly, the educational outcomes of the major inroads toward market-based education do not support the theory that the privatizers are working toward either educational equity or school improvement. Or, if they are, that they are any better suited for this task than are local school districts. If anything, market involvement in public education has worsened outcomes for the most vulnerable populations, increased segregation, and exacerbated the racial achievement gap.

The growing charter school movement has taken a definitive step toward the privatization of education. Unfortunately, the promised transformation of schooling is nowhere to be seen, as charters are not outshining traditional public schools. Charter schools, which can be run by private, even profit-making entities, receive public money that comes from the local school district.

They are freed from many of the regulations governing traditional public schools (like the union contract), in return for the commitments made in their charters (generally related to achievement). Student performance in these schools varies widely, but overall averages for charters nationwide are much the same as those for traditional neighborhood schools (Center for Research on Educational Outcomes, 2009). Nationally, charter schools do not have representative enrollments of students receiving free and reduced lunch, are more segregated than neighborhood schools in every state (Frankenberg, Siegel-Hawley, & Wang, 2010), and do not enroll the same proportion of English language learners (Multicultural Education, Training & Advocacy, 2009) or special education students (Finnegan et al., 2004). Since they are serving fewer of the students with the highest needs, it is somewhat surprising that their performance isn't significantly stronger than that of neighborhood schools.

About 20% of charter schools are run by Education Management Organizations (EMOs), more than half of which are for-profit entities (Finnegan et al., 2004). Because charter schools are publicly funded, this means that a substantial amount of taxpayer money is paying for profits on the education of our young people. Even though charter schools pay their teachers lower salaries for longer working hours, administrative expenditures are between $150 and $800 higher per pupil (Nelson et al., 2003)—with the highest costs at EMO-run charters. As more schools close in Chicago, families are finding themselves with little choice but to enroll in a charter school. There, some are finding that they are a source of revenue for the schools. One charter network in Chicago collected $200,000 in fines for disciplinary infractions as minor as having untied shoelaces (Ahmed-Ullah, 2012).

As capitalistic as the above might sound, it isn't the closest we have come to privatization. A less popular, if more aggressive, approach has come in the voucher movement. Described by proponents as offering choice to families who are dissatisfied with their local neighborhood schools, voucher programs take the money that a district would use to educate a child and allow parents to use it to pay for private school tuition. There aren't as many places in the United States that allow vouchers as there are places where charter and neighborhood schools compete: Only 13 states have vouchers as opposed to 42 states with charter schools. The laws vary in terms of eligibility for students and schools, but

Milwaukee, the city described as "ground zero in the nationwide voucher movement" (Miner, 2013, p. 156), should provide a cautionary illustration.

Here, the program initially was limited to providing low-income children with vouchers to attend nonreligious private schools, which were required to collect family-funded tuition for more than half their students. Eventually the program was expanded and the restrictions eased to the extent that virtually anyone could open a voucher-funded school. A convicted rapist and his girlfriend opened a storefront school called "Alex's Academic of Excellence" (Miner, 2013, p. 212)—just one of several with ungrammatical names. In 2005, when $83 million in taxpayers' money was paid out in vouchers, schools were investigated and closed for fraud, embezzlement, lack of discipline, and not providing instruction. The public schools of Milwaukee, along with the poverty-stricken neighborhoods they served, have been all but abandoned.

Of course, the surrounding suburbs are doing just fine. So it's possible that not everyone finds the situation a tragedy. The children of privileged communities still have good schools to go to, there is money being made that used to be "wasted" by the government, and many of the poor and ethnically diverse students in the city weren't getting a good education before vouchers anyway. We can see the logic in this, but it is an unlovely logic, and it doesn't appear that privatization can have another kind of end result. The wealthy can afford better stuff—whether health care or kitchen appliances. Of course, it has never been any other way, even with the public school system. There never has been equality of educational opportunity for the rich and the poor. With privatization, though, we are giving up on the *ideal* of educational equity. We are saying that it's okay. But for some of us it is not okay. The ideal is worth preserving.

DEFENDING OUR PROFESSION

This is our work as teachers. We need to reaffirm our commitment to the critical reconstructionist vision of schooling, not just in our classrooms but in the community and in the culture. Our role must be to ask the critical questions of just what is the likely outcome of this recent attempt to remake our school system, what are the purposes it is serving, and what is at stake. It won't be easy. The voices that are calling for our schools to be privatized are well funded.

The "reformers" know what teachers would say. The letters and YouTube videos of teachers passionately defending their work and their schools show what side of the movement the nation's actual educators are on. As a preemptive move, those with the means to frame the public discourse have cast teachers as enemy number one—this while the pressure to raise scores on high-stakes tests makes it nearly impossible to teach effectively. Rapid, random turnover based on value-added ratings; efforts to undermine teachers unions and tenure; programs like Teach for America that ask for just a few years' commitment to the classroom: All of these serve the same purpose. If the reform movement is successful, teaching will no longer be a career, but a job—and a low-paid, temporary one at that. For most teachers, neither of these is an adequate descriptor for what is truly a vocation, and the struggle in which teachers are now engaged is for the profession's very survival. If teaching is turned into a 1- or 2-year gig, whether through "save the poor children" service programs or charter schools whose low wages and long hours make it impossible to stay for long, it is our students who will suffer.

Despite the efforts to vilify teachers, and despite the attacks on our unions, on our competence, and even on our characters, families and communities still love and respect their teachers—as Rahm Emanuel discovered during the Chicago teachers' strike. We need to speak to our friends and neighbors individually, and to our political representatives as a group. Having attended school does not make everyone an expert on education. We are the people who can speak most knowledgeably on what our school system should look like. And we are the cadre of civil servants who have been charged with asking critical questions in pursuit of the continual betterment of society. If we are to continue as a profession, if all children are to have a robust and fulfilling education, and if our public school system is to survive, we need to start speaking now.

Stupidity and VAM by Gregory Michie

Sometime in early spring, my 8th-graders' conversation veered from the documentary film we were discussing to the topic of standardized testing. I don't remember how it came up exactly, but if you're a teacher or student in a Chicago school, testing is always lurking close by.

"The MAP test doesn't even test us on what we're actually learning in class," one student protested. After a couple of other students agreed, I told them that their scores on the MAP—a computer-based test known more formally as Measures of Academic Progress—would nonetheless be used to grade their teachers as part of Chicago Public Schools' new "value-added" system of evaluation.

"But wait, what if you don't teach reading or math?" a student asked, aware that the MAP assesses only those two subjects.

"Then they base your evaluation on the average reading scores of the entire school," I said. "That's how I'll be evaluated." Around the room, faces twisted in confusion.

"But you don't even teach reading or math!" someone said. And then several, almost in unison: "That's stupid!" Leave it to young people to see through the insanity of current education policy in a matter of minutes and to state the issue simply and honestly.

My 8th-graders' spot-on analysis that day reminded me of Herb Kohl's prescient 2003 book, *Stupidity and Tears: Teaching and Learning in Troubled Times*. The *stupidity* in Kohl's title referred to education policies that then were just kicking into high gear—policies that valued compliance over creativity, sapped the joy from classrooms, and kept marginalized youth "in their place." The tears were the by-product of such policies: those of teachers following ridiculous mandates against their better judgment or of students subjected to the constraints of a scripted, seemingly irrelevant curriculum.

A decade later, things have only gotten stupider, and the widespread embrace of value-added measures (VAM) for the purposes of teacher evaluation is one of the most obvious pieces of evidence. The complex statistical calculations used in value-added formulas are supposed to isolate a teacher's impact on her students' growth—as measured, of course, by gains on standardized test scores. But there's no research to show that value-added models have done anything to help teachers improve or kids learn, and growing evidence shows them to be wildly inaccurate and erratic. A Bronx special education teacher who scored in the 99th percentile—better than nearly all other teachers in New York City—on the

2012 value-added Teacher Data Reports told Michael Winerip (2012) of *The New York Times* that the data were "nonsense," and wrote a letter with other high-scoring teachers in protest of their use.

Chicago Public Schools started using VAM as part of its teacher evaluation system in 2012–2013—my first year back in the classroom after 12 years as a teacher educator. I was fortunate to join a team of talented and experienced 7th- and 8th-grade teachers, each of whom, in my view, did amazing work with our kids. I worked hard that year to pull my share of the load—getting to know my students, developing challenging curriculum, and trying to teach lessons that were engaging and meaningful. Of course, I sometimes fell short of those aims, but looking back at the end of the year, I didn't question my focus or my effort.

But when VAM ratings were released the next fall, they painted a different picture. My value-added metric was a -0.79. I didn't know exactly what that meant, but I knew the negative sign in front of the number wasn't good. Staring at the score, I felt a bit like Nigel Tufnel in *This Is Spinal Tap* (Reiner, 1984) being asked to explain why his guitar amplifier goes to 11 instead of 10. Here's the scenario as I envision it:

Interested bystander: "What's a negative-point-seven-nine teacher rating, anyway?"

Me: "Well . . . it's almost one lower, isn't it?"

My colleagues' ratings weren't much better. In fact, all five of us—with a combined 85 years of experience in Chicago classrooms and with former students who had gone on to become lawyers, medical doctors, social workers, and community activists—had negative value-added scores. What that meant was that, according to the VAM calculations, each of us had made a negative difference in our students' growth compared with what an "average" teacher might have achieved. Our students learned less because they had us as teachers.

Even if you know it's all a bunch of number-crunching craziness, even as you realize that the margin of error is almost the same size as your value-added rating, it's still demoralizing. And the assumptions that accompany VAM are maddening: that good teaching can be neatly and precisely quantified; that the depth and breadth of a teacher's work can be captured by student test scores; that a mathematical formula, no matter how complex, can grasp the impact of poverty or inadequate housing or exposure to gun violence on the educational life of a child.

The day after we received our value-added ratings, I arrived at school nearly an hour early. One of my colleagues was already in his classroom, as he is every morning without fail, ready to provide extra tutoring for students who need it. Sometimes one kid shows up; other days it's six or seven. Each of them will gladly tell you how much value he adds to their lives. And they won't need any convoluted calculations to do it.

Learning Union by Pamela Konkol

I grew up in the western suburbs of Chicago, in a bastion of conservative values and politics. The irony was not lost on my sister and me; my father grew up in the Back of the Yards, the middle one of many children of Polish immigrants and the son of a stockyard worker. My mother's family left their Tennessee farm when my grandfather, a Marine who fought in Guadalcanal, "went north" and found work in the auto industry on the south side. And although my father's work (military training in computer technology and an executive professional position) allowed him to jump several economic classes from those of my grandparents, to say that my parents were fish out of water in terms of social class and social values in our town is an understatement. But in the spirit of John Dewey, they wanted for me and my sister what the "best and wisest" parents wanted for their own children—they had been socialized to believe that this was where they would find it.

Although my personal story of confronting privilege is for another time, my experiences and understandings regarding work and professionalism—in particular, unions—are important for this text. Although my extended family in many ways embodied "proud union homes," this was not the context of my youth, social development, or undergraduate experience (I went to Northwestern). And as I found out when

I accepted my first teaching position (just a few miles west and a few miles south from both of my grandfathers' homes), even being a punk rock adolescent was not quite enough to fully inoculate myself from the teachings of the notoriously antilabor Reagan administration of my formative years.

Within what seemed like minutes of signing my contract, the union president visited me in my new classroom. I remember smiling and thinking he could have been any one of my uncles (if you need a visual, the famous *SNL* "superfans" aren't all that inaccurate as caricatures). I remember he extolled the virtues of our union, and particularly that our school was an American Federation of Teachers affiliate (although I didn't understand the differences at the time). Immediately, I felt conflicted. I was starting to teach with an emergency credential in a high-need school. I rather recently had begun a graduate program in education and had just enough exposure to the philosophical literature that I found myself at the center of what seemed like a perfect storm of assumptions, beliefs, and values. David Hansen's (1994) work on vocation resonated deeply with me, and as a career-jumper myself, I believed in what he characterized as a "call to teach." I recalled many, often conflicted, conversations I had with my father around his understanding of and experiences with issues of work, labor, and professionalism. I struggled with what seemed like default assumptions I didn't realize I had about the nature and purpose of labor organizations. And every "bad teacher" experience I had in school flashed before my eyes. Join the union? That seemed so, well, crazy.

I was fortunate that the union leaders at the time were understanding of my internal conflicts and, rather than castigate me for not being immediately on board, took the opportunity, as good teachers do, to educate me. They illustrated, without the propaganda I expected given the social and cultural context in which our school was embedded, how the union did much, much more than play the heavy in issues of job security. They helped me see beyond what sometimes seemed like superficial conflicts with the board, and the often much larger issues of policy and practice that were at stake. They helped me understand how a strong union was actually a strong community advocate, and that working in the best interest of teachers was a prerequisite for working in the best interest of the children and families in the community. When educators feel safe and empowered, they are more inclined to take professional risks and engage in the most difficult work of supporting the children in their care. When educators feel valued, they can better embrace their positionality as social agents at the "crossroads of public obligation and personal fulfillment" (Hansen, 1994, p. 411). They assisted me in seeing the union as less of a workforce bully and more of a community organizer, committed to not just the ideas of democracy, opportunity, and equity that I purported to value, but to the actualization of those ideals in our everyday lives. This was a whole new perspective, and one that has impacted my work since then.

Right after the Chicago teachers voted to strike, I posted a message to the Facebook wall of one of these mentors, Nancy. She had passed away not long before, but would have been proud of the courage, tenacity, and soul that teachers displayed. After so many years, it was in these teachers that Nancy's lessons became real. I am forever grateful for her teaching.

SUGGESTED READING LIST

Braun, H. I. (2005). *Using student progress to evaluate teachers: A primer on value-added models*. Princeton, NJ: Educational Testing Service.

This report from one of the major players in the testing industry, with a great deal to gain from any expanded use of testing, nevertheless concludes that value-added models in teacher evaluation are improper use of tests. Braun points out that effects do not equal effectiveness, comparing proponents' interpretation of effects with the common error of confusing correlation with causality in the use of statistical evidence.

Economic Policy Institute. (2010). *Problems with the use of student test scores to evaluate teachers*. Washington, DC: Author.

This report, authored by a group of 10 scholars, including Eva Baker, Linda Darling-Hammond, Edward Haertel, and Diane Ravitch, presents a variety of factors that skew value-added ratings for teachers. Some of these are student mobility, the effect of socioeconomic status on the rate of students' learning, and the fact that low-SES students often experience summer loss, while their wealthy peers gain in learning over the break. These may contribute to error rates of 26% with 3 years of data, which go down only to 12% with 10 years of data.

Ewing, J. (2011). Mathematical intimidation: Driven by the data. *Notices of the AMS, 58*(5), 667–673.

This engaging and accessible essay written for a professional association of mathematicians posits that value-added is the latest in a series of nefarious uses to which statistics have been put. In addition to explaining the limitations of the math used, Ewing argues that scholars have a duty both to their discipline and to society to lobby against the use of test scores in teacher evaluation.

Hassell, B. C., & Hassell, E. A. (2011). *Teachers in the age of digital instruction*. Washington, DC: Fordham Institute.

This somewhat frightening report presents policy recommendations from a conservative think tank. In it, Hassell and Hassell imagine a completely redesigned educational system, where technology enables far fewer teachers to reach greater numbers of students through digital means. The human beings that students interact with every day would, in this future vision, be called "monitors" and could be paid far less than even current teachers' salaries.

Miner, B. J. (2013). *Lessons from the heartland: A turbulent half-century of public education in an iconic American city*. New York, NY: The New Press.

This engrossing work of history by journalist Barbara Miner traces the evolution of school "choice" in the Milwaukee public school system. Driven by resistance to desegregation, the movement has resulted in the expansion of charter schools, the extensive use of vouchers toward parochial and other private school tuition, and a nearly completely abandoned system of traditional neighborhood schools in the city.

Rothstein, J. (2009). Student sorting and bias in value-added estimation: Selection on observables and unobservables. *Education Finance and Policy, 4*(4), 537–571.

This study by statistician and public policy expert Jesse Rothstein explores the effects of nonrandom assignment of students into classes on the value-added ratings of their teachers. Using typical mathematical models for determining these ratings, Rothstein demonstrates the extent of value-added's unreliability for teacher evaluation.

Conclusion:
The Need for a Politically
Engaged Teaching Force

Teachers need to start speaking up about education policy, and we need to start now. We need to start talking to one another about how the "reforms" of the past several years have affected our lives in schools, and bringing our concerns to our administrators where we are able. We also need to talk to our families and friends about educational issues, even if this is going to lead to some strained conversations over the dinner table. The people we love deserve an alternative perspective to the one presented in the media about how terrible American teachers and schools are. Most of all, though, teachers need to start speaking to the public and the policymakers about what is really happening in our classrooms as a result of misguided decisions that have been made in the policy arena. This is a lot to add to an already overwhelming job, we know. Recent "reforms," however, have already rendered teachers' work nearly unrecognizable. Unless we have a voice in school policy, teachers' jobs, at least as we know them, may disappear altogether.

In learning this new work, it may be instructive to examine recent successful efforts to influence education policy. The Common Core State Standards provide a good example. In their analysis of the development and promotion of the standards, McDonnell and Weatherford (2013) differentiate two kinds of learning undertaken by proponents that were critical to the advancement of the CCSS: political learning and policy learning. Attempts at instituting national standards had failed in the past, and CCSS supporters had learned from these failures in both arenas, shifting to "more sophisticated advocacy of a policy idea or problem," as well as in the substantive area of "a policy's scope or the design of its implementation" (p. 488). Because of their political and policy learning, the individuals and groups that promoted the Common Core were able to achieve a great deal with limited opposition.

As teachers, we need to add both of these learning objectives to the already overflowing curriculum of our professional programs. We must become more strategically canny, better at "framing" (Kumashiro, 2008) issues in education in ways that foreground the real human beings whose lives are affected by the policy shifts being considered. We need to learn to use the media and to be of use to the media, providing an alternative perspective to the dominant messages that our public schools are not worth saving. We need to actively counter the widespread belief that just because everyone has been to school, that makes everyone an expert on education. Let modesty be damned—we are the people with the professional knowledge and personal experience needed to understand the implications of the school policies being debated, and we are the ones who should be consulted about them. And if we won't be heard as professionals, then we need to speak even louder as labor, just as the Chicago Teachers Union did in the fall of 2012.

The purpose of this book has been more focused on the second learning objective—a stronger understanding of education policies themselves. We have not touched on every policy or every issue that affects the lives of teachers. Even the selected topics addressed here are not examined exhaustively. Each one is, after all, the sole subject of many volumes in the educational literature. This book is meant to spark interest in particular policy debates and in the realm of education policy in general.

Where your policy focus ends up resting depends on your own interests and experience: your discipline and grade level, the community in which you teach, what is most important to you about the work you do, and what you most enjoy—as well as, and surely not least, the philosophical approach to educational purpose that most resonates with you. If schools, for you, are about nurturing the rich, generative chaos that is political life in a democracy, you may have different policy priorities than if you believe the educational system should help our society run more efficiently and effectively. If you look to education to preserve and carry forward our cultural and intellectual traditions, your policy goals may not look like the ones you'd have if you thought schools should be remaking society—traditions and all.

Regardless of which issues inspire you or stir your passion, we hope that you will keep up with education policy debates and

contribute to the conversation wherever you can. We learned from
the Chicago strike that when teachers speak with parents and community members about what is best for the students and schools,
they are heard and respected. This is your profession, your field,
and your story. Be the one to tell it.

It might sound clichéd, but the future is in our hands. The
struggle for educational equity is bigger than we are, and its impact
extends far beyond the classroom walls. In fighting for a more enlightened approach to policy for our nation's schools, we are fighting for more than what is good for teachers, more even than what
is good for students. The latter is the usual import of the cliché—as
in "the children are our future." While the well-being and developmental flourishing of students is likely our primary and most
immediate concern, more than the kids are at stake here.

In a sense, *everything* is at stake. A review of the four philosophical approaches to conceptualizing the aims of education shows just
how much. If the ideal of the common school disappears from our
shores, the democratic system of governance that has made our
nation great will be in grave danger. If curriculum is allowed to be
constrained by the narrow scope of a multiple-choice test, the rich-
ness and complexity of our cultural heritages, both national and
global, will fade into irrelevance. If schools are transformed into a
source of private profit, rather than our most prized societal investment, many graduates will emerge unprepared for any productive
role in the economy. If teaching becomes poorly paid, low-status,
temporary work, there is little chance that schools will inspire a
future generation of students to change the world.

The fact that young people haven't exactly been clamoring for
social change in past generations (except perhaps parts of the one
just before ours, those who came of age in the 1960s) shows that
the struggle is not just bigger than we are; it is also longer than
we are. The public schools of the United States have been disserv-
ing significant portions of the student population for generations.
This injustice will need to be addressed with thoughtfully considered, research-based policy changes that have educational equity
as their goal. It will be a long journey, but there is no better guide
for it than the teaching profession. Here is yet another responsibility of the vocation.

We know that the policy imperative adds to an already overwhelming array of duties for teachers. We each know how much
work a classroom teacher does, and it is daunting to ask for more.

At this point in history, though, policy work may be the most important of the many extra components of the job. The good news is that it can be fun. After all, policy advocacy is best done collaboratively, in networks of educators, students, parents, and community members. By joining voices to contribute to the public conversation on school reform, we build relationships that energize and enrich us personally and in our teaching practice. It is hard work, but, just like teaching itself, it can be transcendently rewarding.

CReATE and Policy Advocacy in Chicago by Isabel Nuñez

Here in Chicago, about 100 professors of education at universities around the area, including the three authors of this book, have tried to strengthen our voices in the education policy conversation by speaking collectively. Initially inspired and led by Kevin Kumashiro, whose work has been referenced here, we formed Chicagoland Researchers and Advocates for Transformative Education (CReATE). CReATE has issued position statements, research briefs, open letters, and fact sheets. We have hosted public events, led educational seminars, and held press conferences. We have partnered with unions, parent groups, and community organizations. We have been interviewed on educational issues for local and national television, radio, print, and online media.

It has been incredibly frustrating to us that, in this age when every educational practice is supposed to be scientifically proven (read: not the classroom teacher's place to question, and preferably purchased from a large publisher), so much of current school policy has no defensible basis in educational research. Therefore, as university professors, the members of CReATE strive to be the voice of educational research. We make clear what our credentials are, and we provide extensive evidence from the scholarly literature in defense of the positions we advocate. This has been very helpful to the media when they are looking to present a balanced story on an issue.

The work has not been without its challenges. For one, it is all done on a volunteer basis. As hard as it can be to find time and resources for the efforts, it may be even more difficult to negotiate how this work squares with what it means to be a "scholar." After all, no matter how many sources we cite in our publications, this is still advocacy work. We would argue, however, that this is an element of our professional identity that we must become comfortable embracing. Educators, whether practicing teachers or professors of education, are the ones who are best placed and best informed to understand school policy. It's high time we were listened to.

References

Achinstein, B., Ogawa, R. T., Sexton, D., & Freitas, C. (2010). Reclaiming teachers of color: A pressing problem and potential strategy for "hard-to-staff" schools. *Review of Educational Research, 80*(1), 71–107.

Adler, M. (2014). *Response of Moshe Adler to the authors' reply.* Boulder, CO: National Education Policy Center, University of Colorado.

Ahmed-Ullah, N. S. (2012, February 14). Parents, community groups criticize charter schools' student fines. *The Chicago Tribune.* Available at articles.chicagotribune.com/2012-02-14/news/ct-met-charter-fines-20120214_1_student-groups-troubled-students-charter-schools

Aloise, R., Longhurst, R., & Platin, D. (2014). *Report: NYS PTA survey of opinion on the Common Core, student testing and advocacy priorities.* New York, NY: NYS PTA.

American Federation of Teachers. (n.d.). About AFT. Available at www.aft.org/about/

Apple, M. W. (1996). *Cultural politics and education.* New York, NY: Teachers College Press.

Baker, B. D., & Ferris, R. (2011). *Adding up the spending: Fiscal disparities and philanthropy among New York City charter schools.* Boulder, CO: National Education Policy Center, University of Colorado.

Baker, B. D., Sciarra, D. G, & Farrie, D. (2012). *Is school funding fair? A national report card* (2nd ed.). Newark, NJ: Education Law Center.

Batdorff, M., Maloney, L., May, J. F., Speakman, S. T., Wolf, P. J., & Cheng, A. (2014). *Charter school funding: Inequity expands.* Fayetteville, AR: Department of Education Reform, University of Arkansas.

Berliner, D. C., & Biddle, B. J. (1995). *The manufactured crisis: Myths, fraud, and the attack on America's public schools.* New York, NY: Perseus Books.

Berliner, D. C., Glass, G. V., & Associates. (2014). *50 myths and lies that threaten America's public schools: The real crisis in education.* New York, NY: Teachers College Press.

Bialystok, E., Craik, F. I. M., & Freedman, M. (2007). Bilingualism as a protection against the onset of symptoms of dementia. *Neuropsychologia, 45*, 459–464.

Bloom, A. (1987). *The closing of the American mind*. New York, NY: Simon & Schuster.

Board on Testing and Assessment, National Research Council. (2009). *Letter to the U.S. Department of Education on the Race to the Top fund*. Washington, DC: Author.

Braun, H. I. (2005). *Using student progress to evaluate teachers: A primer on value-added models*. Princeton, NJ: Educational Testing Service.

Brickman, M. (2014). *Expanding the education universe: A fifty-state strategy for course choice*. Washington, DC: Fordham Institute.

Brooks, J., & Dietz, M. E. (2013). The dangers and opportunities of the Common Core. *Educational Leadership, 70*(4), 64–67.

Brown v. Board of Education, 347 U.S. 483, 74 S. Ct. 686, 98 L. Ed. 873 (1954).

Brozo, W. G., Shiel, G., & Topping, K. (2007). Engagement in reading: Lessons learned from three PISA countries. *Journal of Adolescent & Adult Literacy, 51*(4), 304–315.

Bruno, R., Ashby, S., & Manzo, F. (2012). *Beyond the classroom: An analysis of a Chicago public school teacher's actual workday*. Urbana, IL: Labor Education Program, University of Illinois at Urbana-Champaign.

Calia, R., Barrett, S., & Valentine, L. (2011). *A financial analysis of the Chicago charter schools: A financial indicator analysis and primer*. Chicago, IL: The Civic Federation.

California State Board of Education. (1990). *Science framework for California public schools: Kindergarten through grade twelve*. Sacramento, CA: California Department of Education.

Caref, C., Hainds, S., Hilgendorf, K., Jankov, P., & Russell, K. (2012). *The black and white of education in Chicago's public schools*. Chicago, IL: Chicago Teachers Union.

Carl, J. C. (2009). "Good politics is good government": The troubling history of mayoral control of the public schools in twentieth-century Chicago. *American Journal of Education, 115*(2), 305–336.

Carr v. Koch, 981 NE 2nd 326 (2012).

Center for Research on Educational Outcomes. (2009). Multiple choice: Charter school performance in 16 states. Available at credo.stanford.edu/reports/MULTIPLE_CHOICE_CREDO.pdf

Chetty, R., Friedman, J. N., & Rockoff, J. E. (2011). *The long-term impacts of teachers: Teacher value-added and student outcomes in adulthood*. Cambridge, MA: National Bureau of Economic Research.

Chicago Public Schools. (2013a). At a glance: Stats and facts. Available at www.cps.edu/about_cps/at-a-glance/pages/stats_and_facts.aspx

Chicago Public Schools. (2013b). Magnet schools, consent decree. Available at www.cps.edu/Pages/MagnetSchoolsConsentDecree.aspx

Code of Ethics and Standard Practice for Texas Educators, 19 Tex. Adm. Code §7-247.2. (1998 & Amend. 2010).

Congressional Budget Office. (2011). The U.S. federal budget: Infographic. Available at www.cbo.gov/publication/42636

Core Knowledge Foundation. (1999). *The Core Knowledge sequence.* Charlottesville, VA: Author.

Counts, G. S. (1932a). Dare progressive education be progressive? *Progressive Education, IX*(4), 257–263.

Counts, G. S. (1932b). *Dare the school build a new social order?* New York, NY: John Day.

Craik, F. I. M., Bialystok, E., & Freedman, M. (2010). Delaying the onset of Alzheimer's disease: Bilingualism as a form of cognitive reserve. *Neurology, 75*(19), 1726–1729.

Crawford, J. (2000). *At war with diversity: U.S. language policy in an age of anxiety.* Clevedon, UK: Multilingual Matters.

CReATE. (2012). *Misconceptions and realities about teacher and principal evaluation.* Chicago, IL: Author. Available at www.createchicago. org/2012/03/misconceptions-and-realities-about.html

Daly, E. J., III, Martens, B. K., Barnett, D., Witt, J. C., & Olson, S. C. (2007). Varying intervention delivery in response to intervention: Confronting and resolving challenges with measurement, instruction, and intensity. *School Psychology Review, 36*(4), 562–581.

de la Torre, M., Allensworth, E., Jagesic, S., Sebastian, J., Salmonowicz, M., Meyers, C., & Gerdeman, R. D. (2012). *Turning around low-performing schools in Chicago.* Chicago, IL: University of Chicago Consortium on Chicago School Research and American Institutes for Research.

Designs for Change. (2012). *Chicago's democratically-led elementary schools far out-perform Chicago's turnaround schools.* Chicago, IL: Author.

Dewey, J. (1902). *The child and the curriculum.* Chicago, IL: University of Chicago Press.

Dewey, J. (1922). *Democracy and education: An introduction to the philosophy of education.* New York, NY: Macmillan.

Dowdall, E. (2011). *Closing public schools in Philadelphia: Lessons from six urban districts.* Philadelphia, PA: Pew Charitable Trust Philadelphia Research Initiative.

Dowdall, E., & Warner, S. (2013). *Shuttered public schools: The struggle to bring old buildings new life.* Philadelphia, PA: The Pew Charitable Trusts.

Dudek, M., Schlikerman, B., & Esposito, S. (2014, March 4). Teachers who boycotted ISAT allowed to remain in classrooms. *Chicago Sun-Times.* Available at http://www.suntimes.com/news/ education/25979696-418/teachers-who-boycott-isat-allowed-to-remain-in-classrooms.html#.VEqu6fnF-So

Economic Policy Institute. (2010). *Problems with the use of student test scores to evaluate teachers.* Washington, DC: Author.

Equity and Excellence Commission. (2013). *For each and every child: A strategy for education equity and excellence.* Washington, DC: U.S. Department of Education.

Ewing, J. (2011). Mathematical intimidation: Driven by the data. *Notices of the AMS, 58*(5), 667–673.

Ferguson, D. E. (2013). Martin Luther King Jr. and the Common Core: A critical reading of "close reading." *Rethinking Schools, 28*(2), 10–17.

Finnegan, K., Adelman, N., Anderson, L., Cotton, L., Donnelly, M. B., & Price, T. (2004). *Evaluation of charter schools program: 2004 final report.* Washington, DC: U.S. Department of Education. Available at www2. ed.gov/rschstat/eval/choice/pcsp-final/finalreport.pdf

Florida State Board of Education. (2012). *Peek v. State Board of Education, et al.*: Action item. Available at www.fldoe.org/board/meetings/2012_10_09/peek.pdf

Frankenberg, E., Siegel-Hawley, G., & Wang, J. (2010). Choice without equity: Charter school segregation. *Educational Policy Analysis Archives, 19*(1). Available at http://epaa.asu.edu/ojs/article/view/779/878

Freire, P. (1985). *The politics of education: Culture, power and liberation.* New York, NY: Bergin & Garvey.

Fuchs, D., & Fuchs, L. S. (2006). Introduction to Response to Intervention: What, why, and how valid is it? *Reading Research Quarterly, 41*(1), 93–99.

Gamson, D. A., Lu, X., & Eckert, S. A. (2013). Challenging the research base of the Common Core State Standards: A historical reanalysis of text complexity. *Educational Researcher, 42*(7), 381–391.

Gándara, P., et al. (2010). Forbidden language: A brief history of U.S. language policy. In P. Gándara & M. Hopkins (Eds.), *Forbidden language: English learners and restrictive language policies* (pp. 20–33). New York, NY: Teachers College Press.

Gándara, P., & Hopkins, M. (Eds.). (2010). *Forbidden language: English learners and restrictive language policies.* New York, NY: Teachers College Press.

García, E., Arias, M. B., Harris Murri, N., & Serna, C. (2009). Developing responsive teachers: A challenge for a democratic reality. *Journal of Teacher Education, 61*(1–2), 132–142.

Gates, S. (2013, May 23). Teacher resignation video: Ellie Rubenstein explains "everything I love about teaching is extinct." *The Huffington Post.* Available at www.huffingtonpost.com/2013/05/23/teacher-resignation-video-ellie-rubenstein_n_3328117.html

Gee, J. P. (2008). *Social linguistics and literacies: Ideology in discourses* (3rd ed.). New York, NY: Routledge.

Goudie, C. (2012, September 10). I-Team: Is the Chicago teachers' strike legal? *ABC Eyewitness News*. Available at abclocal.go.com/wls/story?id=8805308

Greene, M. (1997). Teaching as possibility: A light in dark times. *The Journal of Pedagogy, Pluralism, and Practice, 1*(1). Available at http://www.lesley.edu/journal-pedagogy-pluralism-practice/maxine-greene/teaching-as-possibility/

Guggenheim, D. (Director). (2010). *Waiting for "Superman"* [Motion picture]. United States: Electric Kinney Films.

Hannah-Jones, N. (2014, April 16). Segregation now: Investigating America's racial divide. *Propublica*. Available at www.propublica.org/article/segregation-now-full-text

Hansen, D. (1994). Revitalizing the idea of vocation in teaching. *Philosophy of Education Society Yearbook, 50*(1), 411–419.

Hassell, B. C., & Hassell, E. A. (2011). *Teachers in the age of digital instruction*. Washington, DC: Fordham Institute.

Hinchey, P. (2008). *Finding freedom in the classroom: A practical introduction to critical theory*. New York, NY: Peter Lang.

Hirsch, A. R. (1998). *Making the second ghetto: Race and housing in Chicago, 1940-1960*. Chicago, IL: University of Chicago Press.

Hirsch, E. D., Jr. (1987). *Cultural literacy: What every American needs to know*. Boston, MA: Houghton Mifflin.

Hirsch, E. D., Jr. (1993). The Core Knowledge curriculum: What's behind its success? *Educational Leadership, 50*(8), 23–25, 27–30.

Hodgkinson, H. (2002). Demographics of teacher education: An overview. *Journal of Teacher Education, 53*(2), 102–105.

Illinois Administrative Code, 23 ILAC §228.25 (2013).

Illinois School Code, 14C ILSC §1-13 (2010).

Irving, W. (1893). *Rip van Winkle and the legend of Sleepy Hollow*. London, UK: Macmillan.

Jenkins, R. (2012, May 15). Mamas, don't let your babies grow up to be teachers. *Chronicle of Higher Education*. Available at chronicle.com/blogs/onhiring/mamas-dont-let-your-babies-grow-up-to-be-teachers/31438

Jepsen, C., & Rivkin, S. (2002). *Class size reduction, teacher quality and student achievement in California public elementary schools*. San Francisco, CA: Public Policy Institute of California.

Kane, T. J., & Staiger, D. O. (2008). *Estimating teacher impacts on student achievement: An experimental evaluation*. Cambridge, MA: National Bureau of Economic Research.

Keheller, M. (2014). *New York City's Children First: Lessons in school reform*. Washington, DC: Center for American Progress.

Kirp, D. L. (2013a). *Improbable scholars: The rebirth of a great American school system and a strategy for America's schools.* New York, NY: Oxford University Press.

Kirp, D. L. (2013b, February 9). The secret to fixing bad schools. *The New York Times.* Available at www.nytimes.com/2013/02/10/opinion/sunday/the-secret-to-fixing-bad-schools.html?pagewanted=all&_r=0

Klein, J. I., & Rice, C. (2012). *U.S. education reform and national security.* New York, NY: Council on Foreign Relations Press.

Kleppner, P. (1985). *Chicago divided: The making of a black mayor.* DeKalb, IL: Northern Illinois University Press.

Kliebard, H. (2004). *The struggle for the American curriculum: 1893–1958.* New York, NY: Routledge/Falmer.

Klopfer, E., & Haas, J. (2012). *The more we know: NBC News, educational innovation, and learning from failure.* Cambridge, MA: MIT Press.

Kohl, H. R. (2003). *Stupidity and tears: Teaching and learning in troubled times.* New York, NY: The New Press.

Kohn, A. (2004). *What does it mean to be well educated? And more essays on standards, grading and other follies.* Boston, MA: Beacon Press.

Kornhaber, M., Griffith, K., & Tyler, A. (2014). It's not education by zip code anymore—but what is it? Conceptions of equity under the Common Core. *Education Policy Analysis Archives, 22*(4), 1–26.

Kozol, J. (1992). *Savage inequalities: Children in America's schools.* New York, NY: Harper Collins.

Krashen, S. (2013). Access to books and time to read versus the Common Core State Standards and tests. *English Journal, 103*(2), 21–29.

Krauser, M. (2014, March 21). Bucktown parents furious after CPS questions kids about ISAT boycott. *CBS Chicago.* Available at chicago.cbslocal.com/2014/03/21/bucktown-parents-furious-after-cps-questions-kids-about-isat-boycott/

Kridel, C., & Bullough, R. V., Jr. (2007). *Stories of the Eight Year Study: Rethinking schooling in America.* Albany, NY: State University of New York Press.

Krueger, A. B., & Whitmore, D. (2001). The effect of attending a small class in the early grades on college-test taking and middle school test results: Evidence from Project STAR. *The Economic Journal, 111*(2), 1–28.

Kumashiro, K. K. (2008). *The seduction of common sense: How the Right has framed the debate on America's schools.* New York, NY: Teachers College Press.

Labor Notes. (2014). *How to jump-start your union: Lessons from the Chicago teachers.* Detroit, MI: Author.

Laczko-Kerr, I., & Berliner, D. C. (2002). The effectiveness of "Teach for America" and other under-certified teachers on student academic achievement: A case of harmful public policy. *Educational Policy Analysis Archives, 10*(37), 1–53.

LaGravenese, R. (Director). (2007). *Freedom writers* [Motion picture]. United States: Paramount Pictures.

LaRaviere, T. A. (2014, May 9). Under Emanuel, principals have no voice [Letter to the editor]. *Chicago Sun-Times*. Available at www.suntimes.com/opinions/letters/27339293-474/under-emanuel-principals-have-no-voice.html#.VAEH_FJ0xok

Lewis, H. (2013). *New York City public schools from Brownsville to Bloomberg: Community control and its legacy.* New York, NY: Teachers College Press.

Lipman, P., & Gutstein, E. (2011). *Should Chicago have an elected representative school board? A look at the evidence.* Chicago, IL: Center for Equity and Justice in Education, University of Illinois at Chicago.

Lipman, P., & Gutstein, E. (2013). The rebirth of the Chicago Teachers Union and possibilities for counter-hegemonic education movement. *Monthly Review, 65*(2), 1–12.

Liu, G. (2012). The myth and math of affirmative action. In S. Hughes & T. R. Berry (Eds.), *The evolving significance of race: Living, learning and teaching* (pp. 243–248). New York, NY: Peter Lang.

Lowenstein, K. L. (2009). The work of multicultural teacher education: Reconceptualizing White teacher candidates as learners. *Review of Educational Research, 79*(1), 163–196.

Lutton, L. (2013, May 16). 50,421 Chicago kids in homerooms over the class size limit. *WBEZ*. Available at www.wbez.org/news/education/50421-chicago-kids-homerooms-over-class-size-limit-107196

Mahoney, K., McSwan, J., Haladyna, T., & García, D. (2010). Castañeda's third prong: Evaluating the achievement of Arizona's English learners under restrictive language policy. In P. Gándara & M. Hopkins (Eds.), *Forbidden language: English learners and restrictive language policies* (pp. 50–64). New York, NY: Teachers College Press.

Marshall, J. D., Sears, J. T., & Schubert, W. H. (2000). *Turning points in curriculum: A contemporary American memoir.* Upper Saddle River, NJ: Merrill-Prentice Hall.

McCaffrey, D. F., Lockwood, J. R., Koretz, D. M., & Hamilton, L. S. (2003). *Evaluating value-added models for teacher accountability.* Santa Monica, CA: Rand Corporation.

McDonnell, L. M., & Weatherford, M. S. (2013). Organized interests and the Common Core. *Educational Researcher, 42*(9), 488–497.

McGroarty, M. (1988). Second language acquisition theory relevant to language minorities: Cummins, Krashen and Schumann. In S. L. McKay & S. C. Wong (Eds.), *Language diversity: Problem or resource?* (pp. 295–337). Cambridge, MA: Newbury House.

Means, A. J. (2013). *Schooling in the age of austerity: Urban education and the struggle for democratic life.* New York, NY: Palgrave Macmillan.

Milner, H. R., IV. (2013). *Policy reforms and deprofessionalization of teaching.* Boulder, CO: National Education Policy Center.

Miner, B. J. (2013). *Lessons from the heartland: A turbulent half-century of public education in an iconic American city.* New York, NY: The New Press.

Miron, G., Urschel, J. L., Mathis, W. J., & Tornquist, E. (2010). *Schools without diversity: Education management organizations, charter schools, and the demographic stratification of the American school system.* Boulder, CO: Education and the Public Interest Center & Education Policy Research Unit. Available at epicpolicy.org/publication/schools-without-diversity

Mosteller, F. (1995). The Tennessee study of class size in the early school grades. *The Future of Children, 5*(2), 113–127.

Multicultural Education, Training & Advocacy. (2009). *Charter schools and English language learners in Massachusetts: Policy push without the data.* Available at www.edweek.org/media/metacharterschoolbrief.pdf

National Center for Education Statistics. (2013a). *Enrollment and percentage distribution of enrollment in public elementary and secondary schools, by race/ethnicity and region: Selected years, fall 1995 through fall 2023.* Available at nces.ed.gov/programs/digest/d13/tables/dt13_203.50.asp

National Center for Education Statistics. (2013b). *Number and percentage distribution of teachers in public and private elementary and secondary schools, by selected teacher characteristics: Selected years, 1987–88 through 2011–12.* Available at nces.ed.gov/programs/digest/d13/tables/dt13_209.10.asp

National Commission on Excellence in Education. (1983). *A nation at risk.* Washington, DC: Government Printing Office.

National Council on Teacher Quality. (n.d.). State influence. Available at http://www.nctq.org

National Education Association. (n.d.). About NEA. Available at www.nea.org/home/2580.htm

National Research Council. (1999). *High stakes: Testing for tracking, promotion, and graduation.* Washington, DC: National Academies Press.

Nelson, F. H., Muir, E., & Drown, R. (2003). *Paying for the vision: Charter school revenue and expenditures.* Washington, DC: American Federation of Teachers Educational Foundation.

Noonan, S., Farmer, S., & Huckaby, F. (2014). *A sea of red: Chicago Teachers Union members reflect on how the social organizing model of unionism helped win the union's 2012 contract campaign.* Chicago, IL: Chicago Teachers Union.

Nuñez, I., Mazboudi, M., Fendt, C., Stoelinga, S., & Wenzel, S. (2005, October). *Positionality and qualitative program evaluation: The impact of individual researcher lenses.* Paper presented at the American Evaluation Association Annual Conference, Toronto, Ontario, Canada.

Nye, B., Hedges, L. V., & Konstantopoulos, S. (2000). Do the disadvantaged benefit from the small classes? Evidence from the Tennessee class size experiment. *American Journal of Education, 109,* 1–26.

Obama, B. H. (2010). *Transcript: First State of the Union speech.* Available at www.cnn.com/2010/POLITICS/01/27/sotu.transcript/

Oliva, P. F., & Gordon, W. R., II. (2013). *Developing the curriculum* (8th ed.). Boston, MA: Pearson.

Orfield, G., & Eaton, S. (1997). *Dismantling desegregation: The quiet reversal of* Brown v. Board of Education. New York, NY: The New Press.

Ornstein, A. C. (2015). Philosophy as a basis for curriculum decisions. In A. C. Ornstein, E. F. Pajak, & S. B. Ornstein (Eds.), *Contemporary issues in curriculum* (6th ed., pp. 2–9). Boston, MA: Allyn & Bacon.

Payne, R. K. (2005). *A framework for understanding poverty* (4th ed.). Highlands, TX: aha! Process.

Pearson, M. (2012, September 19). Wins, losses and draws in the Chicago school strike. *CNN.* Available at www.cnn.com/2012/09/19/us/illinois-chicago-teachers-strike/

Popham, W. J. (2011). *Classroom assessment: What teachers need to know* (6th ed.). Boston, MA: Pearson.

Porter, A., McMaken, J., Hwang, J., & Yong, R. (2011). Common Core standards: The new U.S. intended curriculum. *Educational Researcher, 40*(3), 103–116.

Reckhow, S., & Snyder, J. W. (2014). The expanding role of philanthropy in education politics. *Educational Researcher, 43*(4), 186–195.

Reiner, R. (Director). (1984). *This is spinal tap* [Motion picture]. United States: Embassy Pictures.

Rippa, S. A. (1997). *Education in a free society: An American history* (8th ed.). New York, NY: Longman.

Rockingham County Schools. (2014). District home page. Available at www.rock.k12.nc.us/site/default.aspx?PageID=1

Ronell, A. (2005). *The test drive.* Urbana, IL: University of Illinois Press.

Rothstein, J. (2009). Student sorting and bias in value-added estimation: Selection on observables and unobservables. *Education Finance and Policy, 4*(4), 537–571.

Rousmaniere, K. (2005). *Citizen teacher: The life and leadership of Margaret Haley*. Binghamton, NY: State University of New York Press.

Rumberger, R. W., & Tran, L. (2010). State language policies, school language practices, and the English learner achievement gap. In P. Gándara & M. Hopkins (Eds.), *Forbidden language: English learners and restrictive language policies* (pp. 86–101). New York, NY: Teachers College Press.

Saltman, K. J. (2010). *The gift of education: Public education and venture philanthropy*. New York, NY: Palgrave Macmillan.

Sanchez, M. (2014, March 12). To boost teacher diversity, state scraps limits on basic skills test-taking. *Catalyst Chicago*. Available at www.catalyst-chicago.org/notebook/2014/03/12/65790/boost-teacher-diversity-state-scraps-limits-basic-skills-test-taking

Sawchuck, S. (2012, June 26). Illinois preserves teacher-test cutoff score. *Education Week*. Available at blogs.edweek.org/edweek/teacherbeat/2012/06/illinois_preserves_teacher-tes.html

Schmidt, G. N. (2009, September 29). Who created the conditions for the murder of Derrion Albert? *Substance News*. Available at http://www.substancenews.net/articles.php?page=910

Schubert, W. H. (1996, Summer). Perspectives on four curriculum traditions. *Educational Horizons, 74*(4), 169–176.

Skinner, B. F. (1976). *About behaviorism*. New York, NY: Vintage Books.

Sneed, M., Fitzpatrick, L., & Spielman, F. (2014, October 13). Karen Lewis has brain tumor, not running for mayor. *Chicago Sun-Times*. Available at http://politics.suntimes.com/article/chicago/karen-lewis-has-brain-tumor-not-running-mayor/mon-10132014-501pm

Spring, J. (2011). *The politics of American education*. New York, NY: Routledge.

Spring, J. (2013). *American education* (16th ed.). New York, NY: McGraw-Hill.

Stedman, L. C. (2014). Subverting learning and undermining democracy: A structural and political economy analysis of the standards movement. In J. L. DeVitis & K. Teitelbaum (Eds.), *School reform critics: The struggle for democratic schooling* (pp. 45–57). New York, NY: Peter Lang.

Strauss, V. (2010a, October 25). The real effect of teachers union contracts. *The Washington Post*. Available at voices.washingtonpost.com/answer-sheet/guest-bloggers/how-states-with-no-teacher-uni.html

Strauss, V. (2010b, October 27). 7 class size myths—and the truth. *The Washington Post*. Available at http://voices.washingtonpost.com/answer-sheet/class-size/7-class-size-myths----and-the.html

Strauss, V. (2013, April 6). Teacher's resignation letter: "My profession . . . no longer exists." *The Washington Post*. Available at www.washingtonpost.

com/blogs/answer-sheet/wp/2013/04/06/teachers-resignation-letter-my-profession-no-longer-exists/

Taubman, P. M. (2009). *Teaching by numbers: Deconstructing the discourse of standards and accountability in education.* New York, NY: Routledge.

Tennessee Department of Education. (n.d.). Tennessee value-added assessment system. Available at http://www.tn.gov/education/data/TVAAS.shtml

Thorndike, R. M. (1997). *Measurement and evaluation in psychology and education* (6th ed.). Upper Saddle River, NJ: Prentice Hall.

Uetricht, M. (2014). *Strike for America: Chicago teachers against austerity.* Brooklyn, NY: Verso.

Uriarte, M., Tung, R., Lavan, N., & Diez, V. (2010). Impact of restrictive language policies on engagement and academic achievement of English learners in Boston public schools. In P. Gándara & M. Hopkins (Eds.), *Forbidden language: English learners and restrictive language policies* (pp. 65–85). New York, NY: Teachers College Press.

U.S. Department of Justice. (2013, February 6). Court approves consent decree to desegregate Tucson public schools [Press briefing]. Available at www.justice.gov/opa/pr/2013/February/13-crt-166.html

Vevea, R. (2011, October 6). Starting early to create city teachers. *The New York Times.* Available at www.nytimes.com/2011/10/07/us/chicago-program-aims-to-create-more-black-and-hispanic-teachers.html?_r=0

Waitoller, F. R., Radinsky, J., Trzaska, A., & Maggin, D. M. (2014). *A longitudinal comparison of enrollment patterns of students receiving special education services in Chicago charter and neighborhood public schools.* Chicago, IL: Collaborative for Equity and Justice in Education. Available at ceje.uic.edu/wp-content/uploads/2013/11/Waitoller-spec-ed-FINAL-compressed.pdf

Weiss, E., & Long, D. (2013). *Market-oriented education reforms' rhetoric trumps reality: The impacts of test-based teacher evaluations, school closures and increased charter-school access on student outcomes in Chicago, New York City and Washington, DC.* Washington, DC: Bolder, Broader Approach to Education, Economic Policy Institute.

Wells, A. S. (2014). *Seeing past the "color-blind" myth of education policy: Addressing racial and ethnic inequality and supporting culturally diverse schools.* Boulder, CO: National Education Policy Center.

Wells, A. S., & Serna, I. (1996). The politics of culture: Understanding local political resistance to detracking in racially mixed schools. *Harvard Educational Review, 66*(1), 93–118.

Wentworth, L., Pellegrin, N., Thompson, K., & Hakuta, K. (2010). Proposition 227 in California: A long-term appraisal of its impact on

English learner student achievement. In P. Gándara & M. Hopkins (Eds.), *Forbidden language: English learners and restrictive language policies* (pp. 37–49). New York, NY: Teachers College Press.

Willis, G., Schubert, W. H., Bullough, R. V., Jr., Kridel, C., & Holton, J. T. (Eds.). (1994). *The American curriculum: A documentary history.* Westport, CT: Praeger.

Winerip, M. (2012, March 4). Hard-working teachers, sabotaged when student test scores slip. *The New York Times.* Available at www.nytimes.com/2012/03/05/nyregion/in-brooklyn-hard-working-teachers-sabotaged-when-student-test-scores-slip.html?pagewanted=all&_r=0

Zeehandelaar, D. (2012). *A primer on right-to-work and collective bargaining in education.* Washington, DC: Fordham Institute.

Zhao, Y. (2012). *World class learners: Educating creative and entrepreneurial students.* Thousand Oaks, CA: Corwin.

Index

About the Authors

Isabel Nuñez is an associate professor in the Center for Policy Studies and Social Justice at Concordia University Chicago. She holds a PhD in Curriculum Studies from the University of Illinois at Chicago, an MPhil in Cultural Studies from Birmingham University, England, and a JD from the UCLA School of Law. She was a classroom teacher in Los Angeles and the United Kingdom, and a newspaper journalist in Japan. She edited the 2014 volume *Diving In: Bill Ayers and the Art of Teaching into the Contradiction* with Crystal Laura and Rick Ayers, and has published several book chapters. She is an associate editor for *Multicultural Perspectives*.

Gregory Michie is a public school teacher in Chicago and senior research associate at the Center for Policy Studies and Social Justice at Concordia University Chicago. He is the bestselling author of *Holler If You Hear Me* (2nd ed.), *See You When We Get There*, and *We Don't Need Another Hero*.

Pamela Konkol is an associate professor of educational foundations and social policy and director of the Center for Policy Studies and Social Justice at Concordia University Chicago. She holds a PhD in Policy Studies in Urban Education and an MEd in Curriculum Studies from the University of Illinois at Chicago, and a BS in Cultural Studies and Women's Studies from Northwestern University. Prior to working as a researcher and teacher educator, she taught high school students on Chicago's south side and ran an independent record label. When she's not fighting the good fight for kids, communities, and educators, she's active in English bull terrier rescue.

144